for Milt

My friends, money is not all.
It is not money that will
mend a broken heart
or reassemble the fragments of a dream.
Money cannot brighten
the hearth nor repair the
portals of a shattered home.
I refer, of course,
to Confederate money.

ARTEMUS WARD

Contents

Your Financial Foundation, Part I 13
How important is money? How to be really wealthy. Lack of money can cause "heart troubles," too.

Your Financial Foundation, Part II 19
Define what's important to you and put your money on it, NOW.

Dealing With The ET's (Emotional Troubles) 33
Harness your emotions to speed your financial growth. Some simple strategies help you teach those voices in your head a new song. You can start investing while your emotions heal.

Newbies 47
Newbies' "one-paragraph guide to financial freedom." Protect yourself: handle emergencies, market fluctuations, and your job. Tame your credit and taxes. Easiest way to get rich. Would you rather gain 148% or 820% on your investments? The choice is yours.

New Lifers. 77
Why a "New Lifer" can beat the odds. How to make up for lost time and missed opportunities. Simple steps to financial security. If you're going to hit your financial mark, you need a clear target. With these simple formulas, you can quickly design a plan for immediate investing.

How NOT To Ruin Your Children's Lives. 97

The greatest gift you can give your child. Early training for your future financial athlete. Steps for Young Entrepreneurs. The Ben Franklin strategy. Allowance guide.

What About Stocks? 113

Sooner or later, this question is going to puzzle you. Do you qualify? Choose between winners in the Stock-Pickers' Derby.

Debt: When Your Outgo Exceeds Your Income 127

The best debt-reduction strategies. Cutting expenses creatively. Painless ways to save. When credit is your friend. Using credit cards to your advantage. Loans. When to call for help.

The Dirty Dozen Of Finance 153

These are the worst of the worst. All of us have one or more of them lurking in the closet. Evict them now! Monster-proofing your portfolio by avoiding The Dozen.

Home On The Range (Encouraging Words). 177

You don't know how far you've come until you read this. Congratulations! How to know if you're going to succeed.

The Kindergarten Filing System 183

How to find what you need, figure your finances, meet your deadlines, and stop looking for lost objects. These changes can make you money! Pick between ultra-simple and simple systems.

Fine Tuning 199

Special tips and tricks for the truly motivated. Deciding where to put your investment money. Stocks compared, asset allocation, managing five kinds of financial risk. So you want a balance between growth and safety? Here's a portfolio for late starters!

Summing Up........................... 225
Aggressive strategies for wealth-building; start up advice for entrepreneurs. Best bargains in investing. Avoiding financial ruin.

Appendices
   A Business Start-up Advice 233
   B Crib Notes For Comparing Investments......... 235
   C Toll-free Numbers 237
   D Website URLs............................... 239

Glossary....................................... 243
Index 249

Letter Of Introduction

Dear Reader,

If you're a financial rookie, you can learn some money strategies that can save you heartache, bring you security, and help you create a better life for you and your loved ones.

However, timing is everything, and if you're not ready to change the way you handle money, there's no shame. Just put the book away; pull it out again when you are ready.

I don't believe money is everything...although I do think it's right up there with oxygen. More powerful than money is knowledge, because no setback, downsize or Wall Street crash can wipe it out.

Times change. Today's money rules are different than yesterday's. I've made every effort to bring this information up to date. As a teacher and as a financial advisor, I've seen families split up over money, children who couldn't focus on their school work because of deprivation, and anguished people losing out on the life they wanted...because of money mismanagement.

"I've been rich and I've been poor," said Sophie Tucker, "and believe me, rich is better!" I'll second that.

I'd love to hear from you. Please share your success stories, questions, and experiences. You'll find my phone number and address in the back of the book.

Here's to your prosperity!

Coleen Moore
San Diego, California

Acknowledgments

How do I even begin to thank everyone who has made the completion of this book a reality?

Everyone who encouraged me, with word or deed, has my heartfelt thanks. As always, my husband, Milt, supported and encouraged me at every step.

Special thanks to:

Carole Noska and Diane Serns, who goaded me into finding out exactly what I wanted to do, and cheered me on while I did it.

Tish Flemming, who continues to be friend and artistic consultant in everything I do.

My mother, who believes in me wholeheartedly;

Bev Cooney, who volunteered to react to the rough drafts, and pressed me enthusiastically to finish.

Bonnie Parsley, who read and edited every word, *during the holidays,* because she didn't want to delay the book.

Nate McCay, who lent his extraordinary grasp of children and the written word to making the chapter on "How *Not* to Ruin Your Children's Lives" much better.

Marie Fitzgerald and all the group who asked me every Monday night how the book was doing.

Ralene Friend and Jan Serpa, who came through for me in so many ways.

All the clients who shared their stories with me and who are the main reason I wrote this book.

Everyone who carried me through the Second Printing, especially my brother, Jon, and Margaret Ann Slawson.

This one's for you!

One

Your Financial Foundation, Part I

What if you stepped into a football stadium and were shoved onto the field, minus protective padding or helmet? The game is going full tilt and those other players look BIG. They also are focused, competitive and confident.

You, on the other hand, do not know the rules of the game; you didn't volunteer for this. "I'm going to be killed!" you tell yourself, heart pounding. Winning is a thought you dare not entertain.

If you're a woman, you know you're in the wrong place for sure. You didn't play Pop Warner football, attend training camp or learn the plays. The quarterback is shouting some numbers and you have no idea how they relate to you.

Well, welcome to Financial Football, or the Money Game.

No one would expect a novice to do well in football, real or financial, with those handicaps. Yet some of us are ushered into the Money Game with as little preparation or support.

13

Some of us received some coaching from parents, but there is a generation gap.

This is not your parent's financial world, no matter when you were born. We have opportunities...and pitfalls...they never imagined. This book is about *today's* money rules.

The basic premise of this book is that you're an intelligent person who isn't a whiz at managing your money. You may have made a late start putting money away for retirement, emergencies, and investments. Now, you want to do something about it. You may be a "newbie" or rookie, unsure of making your way around the "street"-new to the financial world.

And yet, you must play the game. No substitutes allowed. You can write your own rules, chose your playing field and play a good version of a Money Game that you can win.

The reason that you are the best person to make your own money moves is that you care the most about your own money.

If you follow a few very simple guidelines, you can join the millions of amateur investors who have flooded the market and outdone the experts, in many cases.

You may not want to be a financial wizard any more than you want to go out for pro football...and that's O.K. This book is about knowing enough to get what you want, playing your own version of the Money Game.

Do It Now!

Your timing is perfect, because now is the best possible time to get down to business about your money. You are the best possible person to do it..."with a little help from your friends," as the song goes. This book includes warnings and guideposts about choosing and using your "financial friends." Now is the perfect time to save, invest and transform your money matters.

- Never before has there been more opportunity to easily invest in the businesses of America.
- The economy is good.
- We now know more about effective, simple ways to invest your money.
- The compelling reason is that every day you have your money working for you, is a day that it can grow.

You don't have to devote every spare moment, memorize complicated stock-picking formulas, or digest the entire *Barron's Dictionary of Financial and Investment Terms*. (Go ahead if you want to, of course.)

Speaking of financial terms, I've provided a Glossary at the end of the book with a list of "friendly" definitions.

You don't have to wait for the best time to begin, because the best time is truly *now*.

Get a Life!

You don't have to make money your life either; you already have a very busy life. Money is just a tool to make that life better.

Of course, like any tool, it can become a wrecking bar and do considerable damage as well. This book deals with damage control and rebuilding as well.

"Money is flat, and meant to be piled up," the old Scottish saying goes. This book shows you how to find money, and begin to pile it up.

However, "There are two things to aim at in life: first to get what you want; and after that, to enjoy it. Only the wisest of mankind achieve the second." Logan Pearsall Smith said that. I don't have the slightest idea who he was, but look around you and you'll find that it's true.

I want you to be able to get what you want and then enjoy it! Sound fair enough?

So, in beginning your foundation, I ask you to make a quick assessment of your life's underpinnings, not just your finances.

It's possible that you don't need to evaluate the other important areas, like health, relationships and your mission in life. Maybe they are already tremendously successful and fulfilling to you. Skip the parts in this book that don't apply to you. After all, who's in charge here? *You* are!

However, many people literally can not take a simple money management step because of a need in another area.

Poor health can paralyze you and deplete your savings.

Many years are needed to recover from disastrous relationships. The financial fallout can rival Hiroshima.

I believe relationships are key to the good life. I'll be a contrarian and say that I don't usually advise prenuptial agreements. It's like setting up your marriage for failure. There are times when they make sense, however.

A search for the meaning of life can take you to Tibet and back, often only to find what you're looking for in your proverbial own backyard, or even inside you. Those airline tickets to Tibet aren't cheap, either.

SUMMARY—CHAPTER 1

Building A Better Financial Foundation

- *Manage your own money, with assists from financial advisors when needed.*
- *Start investing and saving Now!*

And while you're doing it...
Get your needs met in:
- *Health*
- *Wealth*
- *Relationships*
- *Your Life's Meaning and Purpose.*

It pays in more ways than one.

Two

Your Financial Foundation, Part II

(Skip this section if you love everything about your life except the money part.)

Lifestyle and Relationships

This is a book about money, yes. But relationships can cost you or nurture you. Those who have satisfying relationships, and that includes the one you have with yourself, are less likely to try to fill a void with overspending.

Divorce, alimony, child support, spending to impress, and spending to compensate for your imagined inadequacies are all potential pitfalls. (That's not a complete list, by the way.)

"When money flies out the window, love walks out the door," say the Irish. How much marital discord centers around money? The *majority* of domestic arguments concern money.

Some of us, usually females, have been sold an image of being a super-consumer *Barbie Doll*. That can be as damaging as the *Marlboro Man* image can be for males. Both of these stereotypes play on addictions.

Men sometimes feel they must impress a woman with the amount they spend on a date, or on jewelry or on status symbols. After all, if you're a good provider what more could a woman want? What indeed?

She may crave caring, respect and understanding, as John Gray has told us in his many books, including *Men Are From Mars, Women Are From Venus*. Money can become the main way to show affection and to attract a mate. It's your choice, of course, but that road is not paved with gold.

A deeper problem than simply using money in a non-productive way is the kind of people you will attract. Unhappiness will follow. Ask Elvis (or his biographers). Does the term "gold digger" mean anything?

Sex and Money

Women are beginning to be less frustrated in their pursuit of equal pay for equal work, but are finding it difficult to meet men's needs for appreciation, recognition, and acceptance.

It was simpler when the man was the bread and bacon winner and the woman was not out there competing with him. She could appreciate his contributions, and he could show his caring and respect for her.

The downside of the current scenario is that when the breadwinner is killed in a crash or becomes the opposition in a divorce, the remaining partner is thrust into the Money Game, unprepared. Chapter 5, "New Lifers," offers crisis counseling, using the equation,

Crisis = Opportunity.

If women are going to rewrite the rule book for the way they play the game, it will involve relationships, cooperation and perhaps less head butting. That means financial support groups, formal or informal, and some new ways of doing business...and of doing life!

Here's an oldie but goodie that hasn't changed. It's one of the most important insights that I picked up from millionaires and billionaires. To get ahead financially:

Spend Less Than You Make

If your initial reaction to that statement is, "Well, duh!" let me assure you that a great many people are not spending less than they earn. They are shocked when they total up expenses and compare them with their income.

Those who take the time to add up their "bare bones" or essential expenses and subtract them from their income may find that some adjustments are in order.

The world abounds with opportunities to spend less, even on necessities. It doesn't have to be constant deprivation, either.

Witness the house sitters or caretakers who live in luxurious surroundings that someone else is bankrolling. Notice how much fun some people can have on little or no money. I used to figure how much we could afford to spend on a party, then have fun creating ways to do it (visit my web page, *http://www.newbiesmoneyguide.com,* and get my *large group for dinner for under $50* menu).

One of my cherished friends, who is an image consultant and founder of San Diego's, *You By Design,* knows how to dress well on practically nothing.

She built her business and her portfolio with her savings on clothes and with other thrifty habits, and still maintained a stunning appearance.

I remember a charming older couple I visited in Rancho Santa Fe. The couple had a problem. They couldn't give their money away fast enough to meet their estate planning goals. They had too much respect for the power of money to be irresponsible about their gifts.

They had already paid for a wing of their church and gifted their children generously...after they observed that their offspring could handle money well.

The day I visited them to offer some financial planning options, the man was gently teasing his beloved wife because she wouldn't purchase a silk blouse that she'd admired. It cost too much money to suit her!

I've dined with a couple who live in a million dollar house and who, one night, afforded me a peek at the stacks of gold bullion they had amassed. They use coupons to save on purchases and they shop carefully, as a matter of course.

Stanley and Danko's *The Millionaire Next Door* is a research-based book that dispels the Hollywood-based myths about rich people. The wealthy have a lot of respect for money, and it returns the favor, by loyally staying with them and working for them.

Another myth buster is *Big Hat, No Cattle: Managing Human Resources* (Harvard Business School Press). If you are more interested in spending than in growing your wealth, you will become very good at spending. You will be a success by some standards. You'll have the life style but not the foundation.

Sooner or later, you must pay attention to the growth and preservation of your money. It may be "later" right now. You *can* avoid the collapse of your financial structure. Decide on a plan, then follow through.

The American Dream

Here's a picture of a hard-working American type DINS (Double Income No Sex) couples. They put the acquistion of money and things first. They may not have much time for family, friends, or even sex, but they are buying the "stuff" of the good life: new toys, fashionable clothes and coveted cars. They are superlative at earning and spending. They don't feel the need to save, because they are good at bringing in money and some can't imagine that it will ever change.

What happens when they tire of working so much and decide to create a more balanced life? All the *stuff* they accumulated will not bring much on the second-hand market.

The DINS have been juggling a lot of balls: career, children, and marriage, to name a few. (Can you relate?) Some of those balls are rubbery and resilient. If you drop one of those, career for instance, it'll bounce and you can pick it up again.

Some are more like crystal, your children and marriage, for instance. One of those, dropped, will shatter and the damage may be irreversible.

Divorce

Here's another picture. Two people suffering the emotional turmoil of divorce are often very vulnerable. It is so much easier to just let the money go than stand up for yourself.

Divorce can be a crisis that threatens your survival in many ways. Sometimes one spouse thinks they are 100% entitled to everything, including all the money. Fighting for money can go against every cell of your being. You need a support group, including experienced professionals.

Finding a decent balance between bringing in enough and not sacrificing something important to you is key to your money management. Usually it requires cutting back on spending, and managing your money well, which is exactly what this book is about. For a foundation, then, look at what is important to you.

Taking Care of Others

Do you want to be a good provider? Great. Just put some into investments. Cut back on the lavish life style if you have to, setting a good example for those observant kids in your life. There's a difference between "Needs" and "Wants."

Do you want to protect your loved ones and yourself and have a good life? Fine. Just save for emergencies, and insure against disasters with carefully selected insurance.

The Good Life

Do you want to have a good life *now*? Super. You can have anything you want…you just can't have everything you want. A money-friendly life style is actually very satisfying. It can feel good to know that your finances are under control, and yet you aren't deprived of what is most important to you.

You pick the things you want that *really* matter, and space them out so that their cost doesn't wreck your foundation.

If you are very late in starting your financial plan, there are some things you'll have to do without. Make your choices so you'll feel like there's still joy and juice left in your life.

Security Today and Tomorrow

Do you want security? Are you a card-carrying member of the "Anti-Bag Lady Coalition" as one of my friends puts it? It takes money to live and have a roof over your head, unless you take a vow of poverty.

If that's not your style, you'll need money. You'll need more than preceding generations because of your longer life expectancy and higher expectations.

We all play the Money Game every day. Think of the last time you spent a day that did not include money.

The problem is that we are often unaware of the rules by which this Money Game is played.

Traditionally boys grow up knowing it is a necessity for them to make money. They usually receive more training in dealing with money and how to obtain it. Although that is changing, girls are not as likely to be familiar with some of the rules. That's a definite disadvantage.

In addition, men and women are different in their approach to the whole game of life.

Men are, in general, more competitive about making money because of their orientation. Sometimes, they won't ask directions...and I don't mean just while they're driving. That can be a problem.

Women may shrink from the Money Game, feeling like an unofficial player.

It helps to realize that money is not a bad thing. George Bernard Shaw said, "*Lack* of money is the root of all evil."

It can be a wonderful way to enhance our lives and the lives of others. It is a hard fact of life that health and education for children in the higher socioeconomic brackets are generally superior, to use just one example.

To succeed at the Money Game, you have to want to, whether you were dressed in pink or blue as a baby. You also must take responsibility for managing your money or it will truly rule your life.

Freedom and Independence

Do you like having freedom and choice? In my experience, the better my finances are, the more choices I have. Is that worth passing by the trendy outfit in the store window or passing up this year's model car without buying it? You bet it is...for me!

What's Holding You Back?

Do you feel like a failure because you have bungled your finances so far and feel hopeless about changing? Don't hide behind that.

"Most of us, by the time we're up on the rules," lamented Pappy Maverick, "are generally too old to play." This book is about getting up on the rules before we're too old to play.

There are financial strategies that work, work all the time, and work for everyone. Try them. At the end of each chapter, you'll see specific action steps outlined: the rules of the game. You can adapt them to fit you.

The chapter on emotional troubles deals with some emotional blocks around money and some transformational techniques to blast them out of your way. Don't hesitate to seek professional help, either.

Some of us have to get really creative to overcome bad early training. Was Hope Steadman, *Thirty-something,* speaking for you when she said, "I think our parents got together in 1946 and said, 'Let's have lots of kids and give them everything they want, so that they can grow up and be totally messed up and unable to cope with life." Read "How Not to Ruin Your Children's' Lives," Chapter 6.

The Road Less Traveled

You're at the crossroads. There's an "X" on the ground, accompanied by a sign that says: "You are here...and you have no one to blame but yourself."

Take a few steps forward.

You can choose between the path marked "Business as Usual" and the other one, labeled "Financial Freedom."

If you're really serious about re-doing your life, read on.

I'll walk with you, hold your hand and I'll even coach you if you give me a call. I'll speak to your group about money and help you write your own rules for the Money Game.

My addresses and contact numbers are at the front and back of this book.

I won't give you money because I respect your ability to work things out and I specialize in fishing lessons, not in handing out fish.

You have to care about your own finances as much, or more, than I do when you embark on the "Financial Freedom" trail. I learned that the hard way.

Once my husband and I decided not to charge rent to a tenant so she could get her car fixed. It was a six months respite. Otherwise, she'd have no transportation to her job.

She contacted me a week after our agreement was made. She wanted to add cable TV to her rented dwelling! We had worried that she would be homeless, jobless and foodless. I guess she was feeling prosperous because of not having rent to pay.

We thought we were helping her; we were really supporting her habit of fiscal irresponsibility. There was nothing wrong that a good emergency fund couldn't fix.

Who am I, and why do I care about your money?

I suppose it all started in Higgins, Texas. My family had two businesses, a two-story house with a big piano, a small plane and various comfortable things that go with prosperous small town living.

In one night, we lost everything but our lives. A twister that still is listed on the "Top Ten Killer Tornadoes of the U.S.A." (Source: tornadoproject.com) hit our tiny town with 261-318 mph winds, killing 181 and injuring 970 people.

Our insurance companies were unable to cover all the losses. I remember hearing the adults discussing their plight, bitterly: "They're paying ten cents on the dollar."

I didn't understand exactly, but I knew it was bad.

Following another twister, which wrecked our new living quarters and most of the airport's small planes, my father was killed in an airplane crash while he was crop dusting.

My brother was born shortly after that. So, now we were homeless, jobless, and penniless without my dad.

My mother, baby brother and I huddled together, living in a storm cellar for about six months, terrified of the storms, the rats and fearful of the future.

Downtown Higgins after "killer tornado"

My widowed mother needed me to grow up fast, and help care for my brother while she supported us.

Then we heard that my grandmother was ill, and needed to make her home with us.

How my mother kept her loving and optimistic attitude is a miracle to me still. I remember my own emotions as anger, depression and fear.

For years afterward, my family, which now included my grandmother, moved around the Southwest. We struggled to exist and recover.

I consider myself a very lucky person. I didn't die, for one thing...and what doesn't kill you can make you stronger, as they say.

Also, I was moved out into a larger world and I learned self-reliance. I wrote an impassioned plea to Arizona State University for a scholarship—which was granted! (We certainly qualified from a financial need standpoint.) Lucky, again!

I started college at the ripe old age of seventeen. It was heaven to me and I probably appreciated it more because it had been an impossible dream.

Education became so important to me, I wanted to make it my business. I was going to be a teacher! That way I could contribute to my family.

My scholarship didn't pay all expenses, and I worked to eat. One day when I was weeping on a park bench over a bounced check I'd written for $1.98...one hamburger...I met my husband-to-be.

We supported each other in getting through college, raising two sons, and building our dream houses.

I took a leave of absence from teaching to work for Principal Financial Group, acquiring insurance, Series 6 and 63 certification. I have been virtually immersed in the study of how to make money and what really works financially for twenty years. I've helped us make a lot of money, made some mistakes...and in the process, learned a lot.

Knowledge unshared is not satisfying. I'm dedicated to the idea of helping people by giving them something better than money: money management strategies.

Then, if a literal or figurative twister blows into your life and you lose *everything*, you'll be able to recreate your wealth and security.

Here are a few reasons why money is my friend:

We watched my Grandmother die, in a county ward where the care wasn't the best but it was all we could afford. Even then, the cost of her care put us perilously close to bankruptcy.

Many years later, my mother and I visited my dying stepdad in a Torrey Pines convalescent center. The best of care was provided, and although he wasn't aware of the lovely flowers and statues in his surroundings, *we* were.

Neither my husband nor I have to work a minute longer than we choose to in our careers. What freedom!

I feel like I can have anything I really want, not everything, but anything. What a glorious feeling after my stormy financial history!

I have a great sense of satisfaction when I pay bills and total up our assets. It contributes to a good night's sleep.

Can you see why I think money's my friend...and why I wish you the best in getting what you want, too?

SUMMARY CHAPTER—2

Building Blocks

- *Big spenders and splurgers are out. Spend smart.*
- *Learn how to play the money game to win.*
- *Money can't buy love, but lack of money can cause heart troubles.*
- *Define what's really important to you; put your money on it.*

Three

Dealing with the ETs

Everyone has emotions about money. Whether you think that it brings freedom, security, and a first-class ticket through life or that it's the "root of all evil," money can get our juices flowing. Watch a game show or trading on Wall Street for examples in living color.

Emotion about money can drive us to work hard to attain it…or to make foolish investment decisions because of panic. We can become depressed, paralyzed, energized, confused, happy, ecstatic and frustrated, just to name a few states the "almighty dollar" can induce.

Maybe you feel money is evil. It's difficult to overcome early conditioning. Bible scholars have turned up many verses to support the concept of prosperity as a good thing…as well as those to the contrary.

However, take a dose of Luke 16:11 to deal with this kind of hangover: "So if you have not been trustworthy in handling worldly wealth, who will trust you with true riches?" …and, call me in the morning!

Cause of Emotion

A childhood trauma or highly significant event can set emotions about money in motion.

I remember mine well. Our affluent family lost "everything" in a series of tornadoes. Our finances were in terrible shape. Finally, it became my mother, baby brother, and me against the world, at least that's how it seemed.

One memorable evening, I asked to buy a Wonder Woman comic book. My ten-year-old soul was filled with desperate longing for it. When my mother told me we couldn't afford it, I exploded with all the pent-up frustration and anger at our reduced circumstances. I threw a fit. My anger hardened into a burning resolve to have enough money, someday, that anything I really wanted, I could have.

I wonder how much self-indulgence I can chalk up to that comic book? I wonder how much of my drive derives from the emotion of that experience?

Maybe your experience caused you to doubt your ability to handle money. Now you're dealing with the ETs (Emotional Troubles) as a result.

A decision made by you when you were ten years old does not have to dictate your moves for the rest of your life.

Passages: Divorce And Death.

Well, isn't life a picnic? I get to be miserable forever.
I'm just going to have to mope and be unhappy and
then one day I'll die.
        Stephanie Vanderkellan Newhart

Is that about it? Is that the way you feel? Here's another take on life:

The longer I live, the more I realize the impact of
attitude on life. We cannot change our past, we cannot

change the fact that people will act in a certain way. We cannot change the inevitable. The only thing we can do is play on the one string we have, and that is our attitude. I am convinced that life is 10% what happens to me and 90% how I react to it. And so it is with you...
                                                    Charles Swindoll

As much as I agree with the impact of attitude, I understand that there is a time when a positive attitude or a cheery platitude just makes you nauseated or elicits angry rebellion. It doesn't fit all occasions.

When you lose a spouse, a way of life, or a way of being, you do go through a process of five stages defined by Dr. Elisabeth Kubler-Ross in her beautiful work.

They are:

- Denial
- Anger
- Bargaining
- Preparatory Depression
- Acceptance

The "death" we deal with does not have to be the death of the physical body. Whenever life presents us its drama, we go through these stages and adapt to them in ways that suit our unique characters. It is clear that all of the stages are dealt with, but not necessarily in a set order.

The lowest point in this process is close to the breakthrough stage of acceptance. It's the winter of the soul. In the preparatory depression stage, we feel powerless; we are in that point of "What's the use anyway?" It is a time of mourning for the death of dreams, hope, future plans, and illusions.

It happens at retirement, or when children leave and business ventures fail, as well. We are thrust into a new role and are grieving, on some level, for our lost selves.

There's part of us that doesn't know anything and doesn't even want to. This part just hurts. This part needs to cry, to scream, to hit something!

There's another part that does know, and is willing to learn. That's the part of you that can benefit from the money management techniques.

It is much easier to recognize that *Crisis = Opportunity* when you leave the stages of grief behind and enter a space of acceptance. After the struggle, one can move to acceptance, rebirth, and a period of increased self-reliance. That's the recurring marvel of life called spring.

ETs and Money

The major debilitating emotions are:

- Fear/ Anxiety
- Anger/Depression
- Guilt/Unworthiness
- Frustration/Dissatisfaction
- Sadness/hopelessness

Most of us have a mixture. One friend of mine commented that her brother suffers from all of those negative feelings, chronically. He has gambled away all his savings and is barely existing on his Social Security pittance at age sixty-six.

Whatever your ET is, it can become an EA (Emotional Asset). Take fear for example.

Fear is usually easy to identify. "I'm afraid..." begins the litany,

"...of losing my money."

"...of appearing dumb."
"...of looking bad in the eyes of others."
"...of making a bad decision."
"...of being broke and homeless."
"...of being on my own."
"...of making a mistake."

And so it goes.

Fear causes indecision. It drives us to look for someone else to handle our money (and probably to have some unfortunate experiences as a result.)

What an uncomfortable, miserable way to feel and live! There is comfort in action. In the construction industry, there is a saying, "Do something quick, even if it's wrong." With thousands of dollars draining away every tick of the clock, any action at least has a chance of solving a problem.

Are you ready to change the way you relate to money? How do you react to that idea?

If you're not sure, ask yourself what will happen if you change the way you handle finances. Sometimes, the answer is surprising.

Some people cling to dependence around money because being rescued financially is the way love has been communicated to them in the past.

Recall a time someone rescued you with money. Ask yourself, "Why did they loan or give me that money?" If your answer is "They helped me out with finances because they love me," and you don't have other love expressions to assure you, you may equate the loss of financial first aid with the loss of love. Figuring out how you feel is the first step.

Taming the ETs

Dr. Phillip McGraw, author and psychologist, offers the strategy: "Name it, claim it, and tame it." (You may have heard him refer to this process on the Oprah Winfrey Show.)

For an in-depth look at his techniques, read his book, *Life Strategies: Doing What Works, Doing What Matters.*

If you're willing to try to rid yourself of your money blocks, here's my interpretation of his process, using "fear" as an example.

First, name your fear, e.g., "I'm afraid of losing my money if I try to invest." Or "I'm afraid of looking dumb if I ask questions." On some level you may worry that if you start managing your money responsibly, maybe no one will take care of you in any way. Is that how it goes for you?

Whatever the reason behind it, identify the fear (or emotion). Name it.

Next, declare your attachment to this emotion, aloud. Admit it.

Imagine yourself going around to your neighbors, knocking on the door and saying, "Hello, I'm _____ (your name), and I'm afraid of losing my money."

Continue your imaginary journey around the neighborhood, going to every house or apartment within your block until you become a little amused and desensitized to your ET. That's the "Claim it" step.

You have just Named it, Claimed it, and now, you are going to Tame it.

Talking Back

To tame your fear, utilize a "Talking Back" approach I first read about in *Feeling Good: The New Mood Therapy* (David D. Burns) a classic book on drug free ways of treating depression.

Here are some facts and arguments to use against the voice in your head that says "What If ..."

"I'm afraid I'll lose money if I try to invest," you worry. Here are examples of possible responses to use when that thought crops up:

- There are some very safe investments.
- I can diversify my investments so that I will be protected.
- Over a period of 70 years, stocks have been the best investment of all.
- Up until now, I may have been irresponsible, but now I'm taking control. No one cares more about my money than I do! I'm not dumb and the more I find out about money, the more competent I'll be.

Talking back to those voices in your head replaces the negative input.

That's the same voice that just said, *"I don't have any voices in my head."*

You are the one choosing what to think, and consequently how you feel and act.

Do you remember this Shel Silverstein poem from grade school? He knew about those voices in the head.

Last night, while I lay thinking here,
Some Whatifs crawled inside my ear
And pranced and partied all night long
And sang their same old Whatif song:
Whatif I'm dumb in school?
Whatif they've closed the swimming pool?
Whatif I get beat up?
Whatif there's poison in my cup?
Whatif I start to cry?
Whatif I get sick and die?...

Everything seems swell, and then...
The nighttime Whatifs strike again.

There are risks in life, but you can minimize and handle them intelligently. Put the "Whatifs" in their place.

Two Sides To Your Emotional Coin

Fear as an asset can translate into a cautious, considered approach. You can use it to get your homework done on an investment, instead of rushing in "where angels fear to tread."

You can look at your emotions in a different way; they may actually be helpful once you recognize them and harness them.

Your fear of being destitute may drive you to do something beneficial about your finances, for example.

Another example of "Talking Back" could take place like this:

Problem...I'm afraid I won't do a top-notch job on my current project.

Voice: You're a flop, a loser. You're second rate. You start off like gang busters, then don't follow through. Might as well give up ever trying to do something excellent. You've never finished up strong or followed up thoroughly in your life.

Talking back: That's not true! I finished college, got a teaching degree. Then I went back and acquired two more degrees. I used them in my teaching, too.

Voice: Those don't count. That was all structured and supervised. You just can't depend on yourself to do it when someone isn't watching over you.

Talking Back: That's not true, either. What about the six licenses and certificates I acquired through independent study? I used them, too! And on one of them, I had to try

three times before I passed. Maybe I am not the most excellent achiever, but I see things through, and I do them thoroughly.
Voice: Well, that was when you were younger and more motivated. This is different.
Talking Back: I will finish. I am more motivated than ever, and the last project I completed was a very good job and only last summer. If I find myself stinting on this one, I'll ask my friends for support. I'm a lot better about admitting it when I need help and about asking for it. I actually will probably do the best job of my life.
Voice: Oh, O.K., then, but I'll be ba-a-a-ck.

Money Manifestation of ETs

Some symptoms of emotional troubles:

- Spending to get even with someone ("He's neglecting me; I'll shop 'til I drop," you think.)
- Spending to escape a life you hate
- Spending as an addiction, whether it be shopping as a hobby, gambling, or status-driven splurging
- Rebellion against past influences...whatever they did financially, you reject, whether it makes sense or not.
- Spending to make yourself feel better.
- Giving up on yourself because you're not perfect ("I'll never get better; what's the use?"goes the refrain.)

Anger often underlies many of those symptoms. It can be harnessed and guided for aggressive money-making.
Depression freezes you in place. You can't make a move. You're paralyzed. Nothing seems worth it. Your finances are hopeless. You're hopeless. If this describes your state of

mind, you're either in a depressed mood (temporary state), or clinically depressed (chronic).

The latter requires professional help. Seek it right away. Medication and therapy can be utilized to help you.

The antidote for a temporary depressed mood is usually action. It needn't be related to your money matters either. Taking a walk is a good example. (Of course, an active spending spree doesn't help matters, financially speaking.)

Sadness needs healing and going through a process of grieving.

Guilt can be replaced with a feeling of worthiness, which is necessary to maintain your finances in good order. Otherwise, you sabotage your own efforts. Association with people and philosophies that nurture self-acceptance aids in recovery.

If you are continually bombarded with a thought, it takes up residence in your mind.... until you evict it and replace it. (Hey, you're probably even letting it stay in your mind, rent-free. That will never do!)

Sometimes these emotions need far more time, attention and work than your finances do. It's time and effort well spent.

Don't Wait Until You Feel Like It

Work the magic of winning financial strategies at the same time. Don't wait until you're perfect to start investing, for example. I'd still be waiting! You may have to "feel the fear and do it anyway." Don't wait until you "feel like doing it." I'd still be waiting on that, too! Do it, then you'll feel like it.

"Name It, Claim It, Tame It" and "Talking Back" are just two approaches for dealing with ETs. Use them, or others you discover, but don't use them as an excuse for inaction in taking control of your money.

I apologize for this pop psychology. View these comments only as suggestions or illustrations. They are not quick fixes, nor are they substitutes for professional help, support groups or growth.

Your Money Needs Attention Too

One of the hallmarks of the fiscally fit is that at least 1.2% of their time is spent planning investments, a little each month.

Of course, planning is only one of the key ingredients to building wealth. The next two chapters supply the other steps to use to create your own wealth and security.

Change and Pain

Change or transformation is not easy. If you're uncomfortable, it *could* mean you're doing something different and effective.

The best comment I've heard about transformation was made by a vigorous woman at a physical therapy clinic where I'm currently "transforming" my back. She and I were discussing pain.

She : "It's a good pain."
Me: "I didn't know there was such a thing."
She: "Oh, you know, the pain you get after you work out, or ski hard all day. It means you used your muscles and they're getting stronger."

When I thought about it, I saw the truth of it. You probably already knew that.

The pain of sleepless nights because you have no financial resources to ward off the proverbial "wolf at the door" is a bad pain, like when I lift something the wrong way.

The pain of doing something new is a good pain, like when I do those exercises the therapist gave me ...two sets of twenty each...and hold them for fifteen seconds., wobbling and straining. That pain means I'm getting better and more flexible.

When I'm finished, I stand a little straighter, feel a little stronger.

That's the way your financial transformation is. You continue to take the difficult actions, maybe even wobbling a little. You realize you are truly transforming yourself, your finances and your very life.

Often, affirmative action in your finances will aid healing and coping in other areas of your life. It is a concrete way to increase self-esteem based on real accomplishment. I believe that affirmations without action, are hollow.

As you're taking the first steps, urge yourself along with upbeat comments. The mind is an interesting thing. It'll believe anything you tell it often enough.

Then, your body follows along the course of action dictated by ...guess who? The voices in your head are actually in charge, I believe. So it profits us to teach them a new chorus, one that encourages us in the direction we want to go, e.g., "You, GO, girl! Call that mutual fund investment line. You're just excited, not scared."

Some Kinds of Friends...

"...are the kinds of friends that we can do without..." a children's song goes. Sometimes, we find that we have surrounded ourselves with a support group of financial dropouts. They support us in the wrong direction.

Create a support group of fiscally responsible people. Use it.

Look for people who are not being hounded by bill collectors or having their vehicles repossessed!

We all need role models; maybe you have avoided the financially fit...*up until now!*

Money rules are pretty simple. "Buy low. Sell high." "If it sounds too good to be true, it probably is." "A fool and his money are soon parted." "Spend less; save more." "Pay yourself first." Why aren't more people prosperous?

Sometimes the leap between knowing what to do and doing it is blocked with these emotional barriers.

Barbara DeAngelis, author of *Real Moments*, when asked if she thought people can change, responded that transformation was necessary, not just change. The difference: "Change is like rearranging the furniture in your living room; transformation is like moving to a new house."

SUMMARY—CHAPTER 3
Your Financial Foundation

- *Identify your Emotional Troubles.*
- *Find and use strategies to deal with ETs while you*
- *take action on your finances.*

Four

Newbies

I heard the term "Newbie" for the first time when I ventured onto the Internet. Old-timers (in terms of computer expertise only) used it to describe an inexperienced person needing help. I've expanded the term to include someone inexperienced in making, spending and/or investing money. This is a book for financial Newbies.

If you are in your twenties, just starting your career, and a "Newbie" I can guide you to financial success with just a paragraph and a chart, *The Easiest Way to Get Rich* (page 49).

The Newbies' One-Paragraph Guide to Financial Freedom: *Spend less than you make; increase your ability to earn; invest; get out of and stay out of debt; protect yourself adequately (savings, insurance), take advantage of tax shelters; insure a future income.*

If you are in your forties, fifties, or upward. Good for you! You will make up for lost time and opportunities with motivation, extra effort and discipline.

That's *what* to do. *How* to do it follows in this and subsequent chapters.

I promised you could solve all your money problems with one simple step, and it's true. Here it is: *Decide what has to be done and do it now!* I'll share some stories of real people who have done it.

Cutting Down on Spending

If you really want something, you will find some way to get it. Desire is the key. What if you want to spend carefully and still include some extras while you're building your financial foundation?

Travel is one of my joys in life. When we decided to go all out for financial independence, I just couldn't give up trips. What we did do was to figure out a travel budget that allowed for our increased investing and saving. We looked for budget trips, traveled closer to home, and cut costs mercilessly in other areas. We knew that the longer, costlier trips were on hold, but we had something definite to shoot for and knew that when the financial " bull's eye" was hit, we could loosen up. Read Chapter 8, to unleash your creativity and cut expenses.

One of the challenges is how to cut taxes. The more successful you are, momentarily, the more you have to deal with taxation.

If you are self-employed, take advantage of SEP-IRAs and use every strategy your clever and helpful accountant can suggest.

Public employees with "non-profits," like public school teachers, pile as much as you can into 403(b) accounts. If you have access to a 401(k), go for it. You'll find a list at the end of this chapter, of ways to grow money faster and face the tax collector later.

Easiest Way to Get Rich

Harness what has been called "the greatest mathematical discovery of all time"—compound growth—and begin saving early. Starting at age 22, put $2000 every year in an IRA that invests the money in a mutual fund designed to track the Standard & Poor's 500. Their average growth has outstripped inflation by seven percent annually since 1926. Leave the money alone until you retire.

By age 65, as the graph shows, these modest savings will reward you with the equivalent of $404,392 in today's dollars, even after taxes.

The sooner you start, the better you will do, because the increase accelerates with time.

SAVINGS

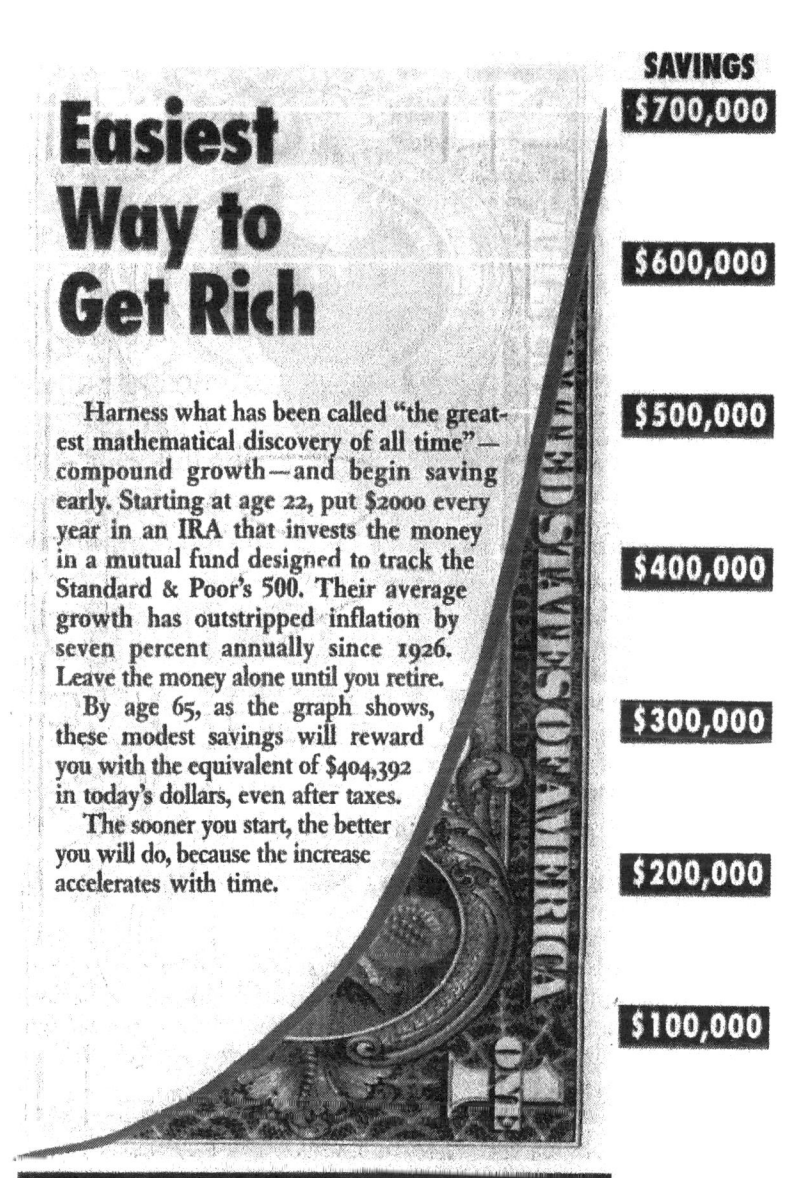

$700,000
$600,000
$500,000
$400,000
$300,000
$200,000
$100,000

0 5 10 15 20 25 30 35 40 45 50

YEARS OF SAVING

Put the maximum amount annually into this tax shelter. (You didn't think the law would allow you to put as much as you wanted in without taxes, did you?)

Don't stop there. When we decided to live on one income and invest my teachers' salary, I was limited to around

$9,000 a year in the 403(b) account. It had the double advantage of being taken out of my salary before taxes were applied to my pay check AND it was not taxed as income as the investment made money. I could choose, to some extent, how the money was invested. Talk to your benefits person at work for details.

When the 403(b) was "full" for that year, we could use other tax shelters, Single Premium Deferred Annuities, for example. You buy them with dollars that have been taxed, but your money grows untaxed until you start drawing it out…called "annuitizing." Talk to your accountant, but get your investment dollars growing in a tax shelter.

Be An Investor: Earn With Few Costs

Saving isn't enough. When inflation is running at about three percent annually, putting $1,000 in a savings account that pays 1.8 percent will actually cost you about $12 in spending power.

Inflation is what is at work when we say, "A dollar doesn't go as far as it used to" or "I used to pay a dime for the movies." Through the years, we've seen costs go up. Some years costs rise very rapidly and then we hear about "double digit inflation"—ten percent or more. The last few years we have experienced slower inflation—around three or four percent. Currently, it's between one and two!

If you, especially as a late starter who needs to make up for years of no investing, don't make enough on your investments you may not keep up with the way your dollar is shrinking.

In case you are someone who still thinks the stock market has a fence around it, don't despair. There are investments that keep up with inflation, take little time, and require only the expertise you gain between the covers of this book to make. You can choose the level of safety, too.

Be an investor, putting a set amount each month into mutual funds. Mutual funds are simply a collection of stocks or other certificates of different institutions or companies.

You can invest in no-load (no sales charge), low cost funds with a phone call and a check, putting nearly all your money to work for you. TIAA-CREF has six no-load funds with $250 minimum or $25 invested initially and $25 a quarter. 800-368-1200.

Consider making stocks part of your saving effort and start investing early.

If you want to invest in individual stocks, please read "What About Stocks?" and "The Dirty Dozen of Finance," chapters that follow.

Mutual funds will work well for the majority and are definitely less trouble. Are you ready to evaluate mutual funds and pick the best among the thousands available?

There's a simple checklist for you to follow at the end of the chapter that tells you how to pick a mutual fund. Another one explains how to understand what is written about them in Morningstar, THE source of information on mutual funds.

It has never been easier to invest in both mutual funds and individual stocks. One of the ways you Newbies are going to make up for lost time is by paying the lowest possible fees with "no load funds" and doing it yourself.

Beware of when a so-called no-load fund has a load. Some have annual 12b fees to cover promotional costs. Switch out of a fund with a 12b-1 fee that is higher than 0.25% of assets after you check on the tax implications of doing so, and find it's worthwhile to do so.

There is a step-by-step guide for you to follow that starts with a phone call, ends with a check, and starts your money working for you…instead of the other way around.

Retirement: Ensuring A Future Income

Not only will growing investments help send you or someone in the family to college and develop financial independence for yourself now, it will promote a prosperous retirement.

Most people working today change jobs so many times that they're unlikely to qualify for a company pension plan—which fewer companies are offering anyway.

Federal studies warn that the aging of the baby boom generation will exhaust Social Security's retirement trust fund by 2036, barring changes. Now that's grim! The fear of the Social Security ATM being closed when you drive up to withdraw money, can goad you into developing an independent retirement fund.

However, baby boomers, born between 1937 and 1961, are redefining retirement. They:

- Expect to live 25 years after retiring
- Will be far less likely to move to a new geographic area when retiring
- View retirement as a new chapter in their life, an opportunity to stay active
- May not retire. Two-thirds will work for the love of it.
- Will benefit from biotech friends' advances (cloning, cyborg body parts)
- Are active, health-conscious, sexual beings because of diet, exercise and attitude. (Sources: AARP, Civic Ventures.)

Can you see any card-carrying baby boomer planning to lower their standard of living when they retire? The average monthly Social Security payment is $780 and the maximum is $1,383 according to the latest government statistics. Could you live happily on that amount? Although there are many retirement calculators available, on line or even from hand-held calculators, you need just a few basic bits of information to figure what you need to save each month: any pensions or Social Security you're entitled to, when you want to retire, how many years of retirement... Figure how long most people in your family live and how much you want each month during retirement.... 80% of what you're living on now is typical...

You can use a factor of 3% for inflation and 10% for growth of savings, or adjust any of these to fit your individual case. Currently inflation is about 2%.

If, for example, you are investing in CD's instead of stock market mutual funds, the 10% growth of savings is too high.

Long life has a downside: rampant Alzheimer's disease, the potential collapse of Social Security, and a crisis in care giving.

Raised with great expectations, boomers won't stand for it. We will need money for that standard of living and for long-term care insurance that will allow us to avoid nursing homes and remain in our own homes and bedrooms—where presumably we'll take a break from Viagra now and then.

Boomers—unless I'm looking at this through rose-colored granny glasses—could confound the gloomier futurists.

Richard Louv, a columnist in the *San Diego Union Tribune*, describes "New Alternatives" this way:

"O.K., imagine this. Big farm house. Led Zeppelin blasting from the mini-disc player.... The scent of incense wafts through the big ol' living room as octogenarian baby boomers swap stories about the 1969 march on Washington. ('I was tear gassed!' 'Nah, you probably just inhaled some bus fumes.') The hired help, a registered nurse trained in aromatherapy and massage, stops by to check the old folks. But basically the boomers look out for themselves.

"They wouldn't be caught dead in one of those old-fashioned nursing homes. Not the boomers. No way. Their kids scattered across the continent, maybe their spouses gone, they come together with their friends to create their own assisted-living commune—one big, happy, or rather hippie, family."

Ridiculous? Maybe not. A friend (a boomer) tells me that she and several friends have already bought a piece of land in the Sierra. "We've agreed that when we get really old—husbands gone or maybe we never married—we'll build a house on that land and live there during our final years."

Another boomer friend started planning for her golden years when she was in her 30s. The SLOP House (Sex and Laughter for Old People) is what she and her friends plan to call their retirement commune. "We want it to be in a college town, so we can have lots of young people around," she told me a few years ago. "We'll set up some little cottage industries and keep busy and productive."

So Boomers could continue to pay taxes and fuel the growth of services or products that assist them. They will not be an excessive burden to their kids as they live longer. "Rock on!" Take *that*, Father Time!

Protection: Increase Your Emergency Fund

Secure jobs may well be history; having more cash is the way to cope with this uncertainty. Sock away six months' expenses available for an emergency.

Even if you're retired on a fixed income, you need an emergency fund. Unexpected expenses like an expiring automobile or a severe illness can seriously deplete your stash. Having an emergency fund keeps you from dipping into the money you've reserved for future living. It gives you choices.

Says radio announcer Daria Dolan, "Keep three months' worth of expenses in a money-market fund that pays a half to 1 ½ % percentage points more than a bank money-market account for example. Put the rest in a three-month tax-advantaged Treasury bill, which pays slightly higher interest. Draw down the money-market funds first when needed. Then cash in the Treasury bill at maturity." You can open a money market account at Charles Schwab or Shearson Lehman or check out Fidelity Cash Reserves (800-544-8888) or Vanguard Prime Money Market (800-523-7731).

If at this point you're asking what a Treasury bill is, the brief and very simplified answer is that it's a short-term (maturities up to a year) discounted government security. You are loaning money to the U.S. Government.

You can buy them at some banks and brokerages for a fee. Make sure it's a true Treasury bill, not a T-bill account, or the interest you earn won't be exempt from state and local tax.

You can buy online, if you prefer. The form is called a tender offer. Instructions on "Buying a Treasury Bill" are at the end of this chapter.

Other Protection

You'll need insurance for disability, accidents, auto, death (if you have dependents). Health, umbrella liability protection and home owners' is often necessary.

When you are in your sixties, investigate Long-Term Care Insurance.

Did you know that Medicare offers limited coverage for long-term care, covering only 6% of long-term care costs, for instance?

Did you know men older than 65 have a 30% chance of entering a nursing home at some time in their lives, whereas for women, the chance is 52%?

If you are your sole support, what happens if you can't work? Disability insurance pays an income while you recover from an accident or illness.

Learn from the mistakes of others. You can't live long enough to make them all yourself. Check it out.

Find an insurance company with good financial ratings and a solid history; get a good insurance rep to guide you to a balance between needs and costs.

Any good insurance agent would be happy to help you evaluate your situation. Choose them as carefully as you would any financial advisor.

Mortgage insurance is usually not necessary if you are adequately covered in the other areas, and is a bigger boon to the loan company than to you.

The computer and the Internet can be valuable in comparing prices and gathering data.

Did you know the online generation's answer to the couch potato is the mouse potato?

Job Protection

Another form of protection is increasing your skills. Acquiring certification and knowledge not only makes you a more valuable employee or entrepreneur, but also broadens your range of possible jobs. It often increases your earnings in your current job.

Take advantage of online courses and colleges catering to the schedules of working adults and those who need to stay at home, the University of Phoenix, for example (uophx.edu), or the University of Redlands (1-888- 999-9844 or redlands.edu on the Internet.).

San Diego offers a plethora of free job preparation and related courses plus vocational counseling. Two of my personal favorites are ROP, Regional Occupational Program, (1-800-479-4900 or (858) 627-7208.) and the San Diego Career Center (858) 627-2553 or iteachyou on the Net.)

The "iteachyou" site is a must for computer Newbies who live in the San Diego area. Check it out!

Go to a search engine then type in "online courses" to search.

Check the list of a few popular search engines at the end of this chapter, as well as a step-by-step Internet guide to contact mutual fund companies.

Wherever You Go, There You Are!

Make yourself a "keeper" on your job by looking honestly at these three personal aspects: (After all, you don't want to get "uninstalled" as the online generation refers to "being fired.")

Attitude Often people are dismissed on the basis of their inability to relate well to other people. Sometimes this problem overrides your competency. Do you listen well?

Stephen Covey says one of the Seven Habits of Highly Effective People is: Seek to understand, before you seek to be understood." Your attitude is key.

Duke University studies have shown 90+% of executives fired in a five-year time period were dismissed for incompetence in dealing with other people, not for lack of job skills.

Image Your appearance needs to be in harmony with your job. When I moved from the classroom to the financial world, I called Diane Serns with *You By Design*, a San Diego image consulting firm, to help me with the transition.

It was fun, affordable and paid off. Did you know that most people decide in the first few moments of meeting you whether they want to do business with you or not? I doubt if the decision is based totally on your IQ or SAT scores.

Extras Your "surprise" factor should be high. People expect you to do certain services, or jobs.

If you surprise them by doing more or by doing the unexpected, you become memorable. I'm thinking of a restaurant where we had a delicious meal, but a friend was disappointed that they had no cheesecake to offer her.

Before the evening was over, she had her favorite dessert. They had it brought from the deli down the street! We raved about that restaurant for weeks. That's the "surprise factor" at work.

What does that have to do with money? Unemployment is hard on your bank account! Avoid it whenever possible. (At least until you've saved enough to be totally independent.)

Someday you'll want to choose whether to work or not.

Retirement is drastically different than it used to be. People are starting new careers and living active lives which demand more money.

Often, senior citizens are sandwiched between the needs of young adult children and the needs of parents. Directly or indirectly, your finances are impacted. All the more reason to save and invest, vigorously, NOW.

Tax Defense

Minimize your state and local taxes as well as your federal income taxes.

Never lie to your mother or to the Internal Revenue Service. Use every lawful strategy you can to avoid taxes, but don't cheat. They'll find out.

I know a young woman who is still trying to explain to IRS agents why she "allowed" her ex-husband to evade income taxes totally and illegally for several years. Since they can't find him, they are looking for answers...and money...from her. Call your congressman for help!

Besides cheating on your return or evading taxes, there are honest, intelligent strategies to reduce your taxes. It's worth while to search for them, hand-in-hand with an accountable accountant. For example, invest in a mutual fund in the first part of the year, not the end. Otherwise you'll be docked for gains you haven't fully realized. It's like having a hangover for a party you didn't attend.

When you realize how much of your money goes for taxes, you will be motivated to pay your fair share...and not one penny more!

Contact a representative for the Big Three Least Favorite Ways to Spend Money: Taxes, Insurance and Interest Payments. Spend some time with these experts, enlisting them in your quest to lower the amount of money you spend. It's worth the time and money, if you have to pay for it. Accountants, insurance agents, and mortgage brokers can help you if you take a proactive stance.

There's a time when frugality doesn't pay...like when you save money by going to the "Best Guess Discount Accounting" and see posted on their door, "EIGHT CONTINUOUS DAYS WITHOUT A SUBPOENA!"

In 1980 to 1993, the average federal income tax bite rose about 6 percent. State income taxes, by contrast, have shot up more than 40 percent over that same period, and local taxes have risen sharply, too. These trends seem likely to continue.

To live comfortably once you stop working, you'll need an annual income equal to 75-80 percent of your current income.

Taxes and Retirement

Do you suppose there's a reason why the states with the lowest income tax tend to have heavier concentrations of retirees? Some states tax Social Security income; others, don't. If they also boast a lower cost of living, the draw is accentuated.

The Third Edition of John Howells' *Where To Retire...America's Best and Most Affordable Places* is one of the best guides to retirement places.

Write The Globe Pequot Press, Dept. FIL, P.O. Box 833, Old Saybrook, CT 06475 for a copy, if you can't find it anywhere else.

The states without individual income taxes are Alaska, Florida, Nevada, South Dakota, Texas, Washington and Wyoming. Don't be too quick to rejoice; higher property taxes and sales taxes will make up the deficit. (See "Relative Tax Burdens In Choice Retirement States.)

Relative Tax Burdens in Choice Retirement States
(Ranked from lowest to highest)

1. Alabama	13. Florida
2. Arkansas	14. New Mexico
3. Utah	15. Missouri
4. Washington	16. Georgia
5. Tennessee	17. Nevada
6. Oklahoma	18. Virginia
7. Kentucky	19. Oregon
8. Texas	20. California
9. Mississippi	21. Colorado
10. South Carolina	22. Arizona
11. Louisiana	23. Hawaii
12. North Carolina	

Source: Advisory Commission of Intergovernmental Relations

Real Estate

Consider buying a house or condo instead of renting. It has some tax advantages, loan possibilities, and you end up with something to show for your money besides rent receipts. (See Chapter 12, "Fine Tuning.")

You can find a foreclosed home at the Web sites of Fannie Mae, www.fanniemae.com and Freddie Mac, www.freddiemac.com .

Foreclosed homes can be less expensive than others in the same neighborhood, but they may be in poor condition. Local real estate agents, banks, and lenders can also help you find foreclosures in your area.

Houses have some pitfalls. They tempt you to spend and the last thing you want to do is buy a house that needs costly, unexpected repairs. (Have you seen the comedy "The Money Trap?" We were remodeling a fixer home we had purchased when I saw it. I laughed too hysterically at their mishaps. We were living them.) See "Big Home Defects And How To Uncover Them," page 73.

Don't neglect the intangibles, either. Ask about the schools; be alert for graffiti. Talk to the neighbors about the quality of life in the area.

Debt

I've devoted a chapter to this subject. Some basics include:

- Pay off your credit cards and cut up the ones you can do without. Paying off high-interest credit cards is one of the wisest moves you can make today.
- The hottest new investment tip: Spend less.
- Keep one credit card for emergencies; pay cash.
- Refinance your high-rate credit cards and student loans
- Find low cost auto loans and mortgages.

Here are some help items for each of the action steps mentioned above.

Automatic Investment Plan

Don't waste time waiting for the perfect moment to make your leap into a mutual fund. Use a simple investing technique called dollar cost averaging

You invest a fixed amount, say $250, every month, whether the price of the shares you're buying is going down or up. The best time to get into investing is NOW. Buying this way, you're more likely to acquire more shares at median, rather than high prices.

Simply arrange an automatic transfer between your bank and a mutual fund. Or authorize payroll deductions. The same amount of money will be withdrawn from your bank account specified date and transferred to the fund of your choice.

To arrange, call the 800 number of the fund you've chosen and ask for the forms for automatic investing. Usually they ask only for a voided check and for some information. (See "Picking a Mutual Fund," page 65).

You can do dollar-cost averaging with a lump sum from an inheritance or a pension plan distribution. Invest part of the money in regular installments. Bank the uninvested portion in a money market account.

Check the amount you're investing at least annually, to adjust for salary increases and inflation

Total Return, January 1984-December 1997

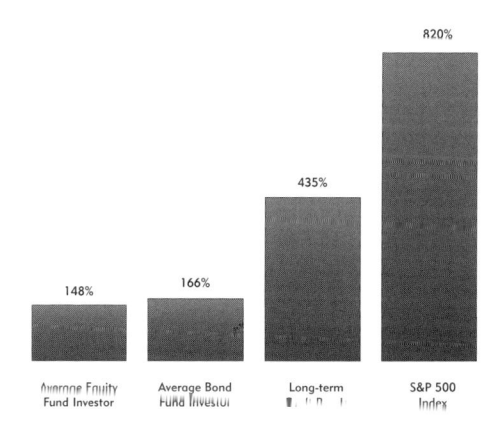

Average Equity Fund Investor	Average Bond Fund Investor	Long-term	S&P 500 Index
148%	166%	435%	820%

A buy-and-hold investor in an S&P 500 fund, who left the money alone to grow would have realized returns much higher than the average investor over the period from January 1984 to December 1997.

You are making up for lost time; put as much in as you possibly can. You want your money to start working for you, instead of you working for money.

Would you rather make 148 percent on your money or 820 percent?

Take a look at the results of a DALBAR study on page 63! The graph shows the total return over a thirteen-year period of a fund investing in the S&P 500 stocks.

Average investors who skipped around from fund to fund made an average of 148 percent on their investments, an average of about 11 percent a year. That's not bad, which is why stocks are in such favor. But the ones who didn't dance from one highly touted stock or fund to another in that same period made 820 percent, almost 6 times better return than the average investor.

Many investors buy emotionally, when a stock or fund is in favor...translation: it costs a lot. When the news turns sour, driving the price down, they sell. Factor in the cost of buying and selling...translation: commissions and taxes... and you can see why the standpatters fared so much better.

Buying a Treasury Bill.

- Fill out the tender form, obtained from the Internet site (See Appendix D) and enclose payment for the full face amount of the security. There's no service charge.
- Pay with a certified personal check, cashier's check or Treasuries you own that will mature by the new issue date. Make your check payable to the Federal Reserve Bank or Branch to which you're submitting your tender. If your tender is going directly to the Treasury, your check must be made payable to the Bureau of the Public Debt.

- Where the form asks "Bid Type," check the box labeled "Noncompetitive," meaning you'll accept the average auction price.
- In the section headed "Direct Deposit Information," write your bank's nine-digit identifying number in the space labeled "Routing Number" (found at the bottom of your check or deposit slip). Then list the name of your bank, your account number, and the name on your account.
- Write on the envelope that this is a "Tender for Treasury Securities"
- Mail your tender form and check or the Federal Reserve Bank (or Branch) or to the Bureau of the Public Debt, Washington D.C. 20239-1500.

Picking A Mutual Fund

Here's how (assuming you're a fairly conservative investor):

- Go to the library and ask for a copy of Morningstar Mutual Funds, a loose-leaf reference book that lists thousands of funds, giving each a rating of one to five stars..five being the best. (You can access their web site by typing morningstar in the location box on the Internet.

Much of their information is free; they charge $1.50 for a detailed report on a fund, or copy the same information for less at the library.)

- If you have a particular fund in mind, look it up. The handy one-page synopsis starts with a straightforward description of the fund. It will talk about whether the fund seeks "capital apprecia-

tion"—growth of your principal—or income. You want a fund that seeks both...since one provides more stability, the other represents greater potential for profit.
- Look for a fund that invests in preferred stocks and bonds as well as common stocks. A good balanced fund is unlikely to use "leverage," a practice that allows the fund manager to borrow additional money to invest. Here's an example of a fund called "Founders Special" an aggressive growth fund: "The fund engages in aggressive techniques, such as leveraging and short-term trading. It may invest up to 30 percent of assets in foreign stocks." If you are conservative, this is not for you.
- Look at the 10-year history (one of the description's most valuable sections), which shows the fund's performance in each of the past 10 years. You can see how volatile (how much the price varies) a fund is and compare its performance to that of the market as a whole as measured by Standard & Poor's 500.
- Pay particular attention to comparison to its peers—other funds of the same type—it should do better on both counts.
- See if the same fund manager has been with the fund during the ten years, or how it has done during his tenure. You can eliminate lots of research by simply picking a no-load index 500 fund. (See the list on page 67.) They are not actively managed, and yet have an impressive record, usually beating the returns of the managed funds.
- Check the costs of your fund (No-load is best; never pay over 3%).

- Look for a fund with a low turnover ratio. It costs you money for every transaction, one way or another. That's another advantage index funds have.
- When you have identified a promising fund, call the fund's toll-free number and ask for a prospectus (or download it from your computer). You can usually type in the fund name with no capital letters, e.g. fidelity or vanguard, and go to their site. If you like, look up the fund's net asset value (the price per share) in the newspaper and watch it for a few weeks.

    Another good resource is S&P's Personal Wealth web site, personalwealth.com, that allows you to compare the fund you're interested in with another fund or index.
- When you're ready to invest, call the fund company and ask if they'll waive the usual minimum purchase if you agree to invest a regular amount—say $100—every month. You'll pay less on average for your shares by buying them at regular intervals

Low-Cost No-Load Index Funds, S&P 500

Fund Name	Symbol	Phone 1-800	Expense Ratio
USAA 500 Index	USSPX	383-8722	0.18%
Vanguard S&P 500	VFINX	871-3879	0.19%
Fidelity Spartan Market	FUSEX	544-8888	0.19%
T. Rowe Price Equity Index*	PREIX	638-5660	0.40%
Strong Index 500*	SINDX	359-3379	0.45%

*Funds with low minimum investment.
See indexfundsonline.com for a complete list.

regardless of whether the price is up or down. The principle involved is called "dollar cost averaging.

Understanding Morningstar

Often Newbies are referred to Morningstar as a good source of information about mutual funds. Then we go to the trouble of tracking down a report...only to find it's written in what seems to be English, but looks so intimidating we feel like heading to the Horror section of the library for comfort (or the Solitaire game on the computer).

Actually, you can get all the information you really need in seven small spots on the report. You can handle seven, right? Here they are:

1. How many "stars" does it rate? You'll find them about the middle of the report, on top. Each fund has one to five stars based on returns and risk. Five is best. With as many funds as there are, why bother with any that have less than three?

2. What type of fund is it? Morningstar analyzes whether the fund does what the prospectus advertises. (Top right)

3. Who's in charge here? Look to see if a new manager might steer the fund in a new direction. (Left side)

4. What does an expert think? An analyst reviews fund problems and successes. (Bottom left)

5. How does the fund compare? See at a glance how the fund has performed vs. similar funds. (Right, second section)

6. How has the fund done? Check the fund's returns over various time periods and compare that with S&P 500 Index or appropriate benchmarks. (Left, middle)

7. What does the fund own? Evaluate your comfort with this mix of stocks, bonds and cash. (Middle, right)

Emergency Fund Savings

Figure how much it would cost you to live for six months. That's your goal for this account.

Ideally, you will have this savings in a money market mutual fund, earning more than inflation. It is safe and you can get your money without penalty.

If you are trying to manage investing and saving both, build this fund up first.

One option that is slightly riskier is to put this money into an index fund that is not a tax shelter and let it serve as both an investment and savings. When the target amount is reached, you can transfer it to a money market mutual fund. In extreme cases, the money serves as a self-insurance in case of disability. As soon as you can, look into disability insurance, however. Six months expenses can evaporate quickly in the wake of a serious illness or accident.

Insurance And Protection

Start with your own preventative medicine. Look at your family's health history. Take steps to eliminate or minimize risks.

For example, osteoporosis runs in my family. I took calcium and did weight-bearing exercise. I had a baseline bone density test to compare to subsequent annual scans.

When a problem was identified and I found out I was losing bone tissue in spite of my efforts, I went to a specialist, who prescribed a new drug. Thanks to the efforts of all concerned, I tested normal last time!

If you are getting a divorce, read the check list "Maintaining Your Health Insurance After Divorce," page 71.

- Do the same kind of assessment and take preventative action to safeguard property, e.g. installing alarms and clearing brush away from your property.
- If you have dependents, get term life insurance. Make sure your insurance company has the highest financial stability rating. (More detail in later chapters.)
- Write a will, no matter how crude or simple...or do it "right" by consulting an attorney, but do it.
- You'll also need two Power of Attorney documents, one for business (in case you are unable to conduct your own) and one for Health Care (giving power to someone to make life-and-death decisions in case you're unable to do so).
- Non-profit memorial societies provide really low cost services and you get to describe your wishes regarding services, cremation or burial, etc. and save your loved ones the strain of decision-making.

Non-profit societies don't advertise much; one example is San Diego Memorial Society (858) 874-7921.

- Check your employee benefits, if any, especially disability insurance Don't depend on social security disability; their definition of disabled is almost impossible to meet unless you're an extreme case.
- Purchase disability insurance if you are your sole support.
- Health Insurance benefits are important job benefits. If you are retired, you will need Medicare B (for a small fee) and a so-called "Medigap" insurance to supplement the Medicare and no-cost Medicare A plans. Get quotes on the Internet. Two

sites are: financial-wizard.com and health.yahoo.com.
- Newbies approaching their sixties should investigate Long Term Care Insurance plans. It takes a hefty bank roll to support a lingering illness or condition. Cost is prohibitive for someone starting insurance in later years.
- Evaluate insurance of possessions, auto, house, renter's for possible discounts, lower costs, adequate coverage—but no overlapping coverage.
- Avoid mortgage insurance and extended warrantees.
- Consider umbrella liability coverage if you have a lot to lose in case of a law suit, or are in a high risk situation.

Maintaining Your Health Insurance After Divorce

If your health insurance is through your spouse's employer, once the divorce is final you will need to obtain health insurance.

Deal with this issue early in divorce negotiations, so that there is no gap in coverage.

If your spouse works for a company that employs 20 or more people, then you are eligible to apply for continued coverage under a Federal law known as "COBRA" (Consolidated Omnibus Budget Reconciliation Act, not a snake.)

Notify your spouse's employer within 60 days of becoming divorced. Otherwise, you will not be eligible.

If your employer provides health insurance for you at little or no charge to you, take it. You are responsible for the entire amount of the premium under COBRA.

If you can't get it through your employer, check out private plans such as Blue Cross to compare benefits and the cost.

Ask the personnel at your doctors' offices what insurance plans they accept and which ones make payments that are most hassle-free.

COBRA plans are not permanent. Find out how long the coverage lasts for you. (I've heard 18-36 months, varying with the situation and source.) Take a private plan if you are healthy. You are protected from becoming uninsurable; it may be less expensive. If you opt for the COBRA coverage, remember to be shopping for health insurance or campaigning for coverage at work, if possible.

A Few Popular Search Engines On The Internet

A search engine is simply a screen on the Internet that you visit to help you find information. When you type the above address in the location box of your screen, once you've signed online, you will see a place labeled SEARCH to type your subject of interest.

Yahoo <www.yahoo.com>
- Subject guide and free-text (every word on a page)
- Free text searching of the WWW. Lets you type in your question.

Alta Vista <www.altavista.com>
- Free text searching of the WWW. Lets you type in your question.

Google <www.google.com>
- Results based on an analysis of a page's popularity.

Excite <www.excite.com>
- Concept searching.

Hot Bot <www.hotbot.com>
- Lets you limit search to pages with certain features, e.g., graphics, sound.

Dog Pile <www.dogpile.com>
- Combines major search engines.

Mutual Fund Information on the Internet

1. Get on the Internet.
2. Highlight the address in the Location box so you can type a new address by clicking on it. This directs where you go on the Internet.
3. Type the name of your mutual fund company, without a capital letter, e.g. janus or vanguard.
4. Press the "Enter" key on your computer keyboard.
5. Choose the information by clicking on it.
6. You can order a prospectus, print forms, obtain contact numbers, and other information.

Big Home Defects And How To Uncover Them

- Tilted floor. Place a large marble in each corner of a room with a hard floor surface—no carpeting. If the marble rolls to the other side, the house may be sinking on one side. REPAIR COST: As much as $15,000 to $25,000 average.
- Crumbling foundation. A hairline crack is just another crack. But a V-shaped crack means that the foundation is literally pulling apart. REPAIR COST: a few thousand up to $15,000.
- Separations in floor under carpeting Walk in your stocking feet. If you feel a crack, ground movement may have broken the slab. REPAIR COST: Only

around $100 if the problem is cosmetic;$15,000 or more to lay a new slab and foundation.
- Holes in the roof. Go to the attic and look up at the roof on a sunny day. Pinpoints of light, like a starry night, means the underlayment is worn out. REPAIR COST: $5,000 and up.
- Worn-out roof. Look for curling ends on fiberglass/asbestos shingles. Also, look for signs of water damage on inside ceilings. REPAIR COST: $3,000 and up. Patching may not work.
- No ground wire at electrical outlets. The outlets in the kitchen and bathrooms have only two holes, instead of three. REPAIR COST: $1,000 TO 3,000 for rewiring to bring up to modern codes.

See *Tips and Traps When Buying a Home* by Robert Irwin for more information.

Chapter 4—Summary

Financial Freedom: Action Steps

- *Set up an automatic investment plan.*
- *Fund tax shelters first.*
- *Fund savings for emergencies. Protect job.*
- *Reduce insurance, taxes and living costs by shopping around.*
- *Pay off credit cards. Cut down on number of cards.*

Five

New Lifers

How to Make Up for Lost Time and Opportunities

New Lifers...either you know one or you are one. Am I talking to you? Here's a profile of a "New Lifer :

You have undergone a drastic life passage in the proceeding few years, like divorce, the death of a spouse, or a particularly meaningful birthday.

You have successfully avoided learning anything about finances... up until now... and you are highly motivated because something similar to a biological clock is going off like a shrill alarm inside your body and brain.

You decide to make some dramatic changes, especially in your personal finances.

The bad news is: you have a challenge, because time is not on your side.

The good news is: you have a powerful, urgent motivation, which is to your advantage. That alarm is hard to ignore. Wake up and smell the coffee!

You are *me*, a few years ago, so I can speak most tenderly and knowledgeably to you. As a New Lifer myself, I'm revisiting an old neighborhood. I can tell you how to get from here to there on your way to Easy Street.

Finding Money

Now is a good time to deal with that "But-you-don't-understand-I-can't-even-make-all-my-payments...much less save anything." Let me ask you this: How much money, each week, do you suppose you can't really account for, but you do spend? $10? $25? Most of us can admit to that amount.

Can you entertain a small hope that under a new system of money management, more funds will be made available to you for investing? That's a "giant leap" ahead, on your path to financial security.

Most people estimate that an average of $100 a month slips away from them, somehow. Grab that slippery sum and fasten a leash around it, like you would a frisky dog. Bring it along on your walk.

In addition, you can develop a plan by analyzing your expenditures. Maybe you will skip the café lattes ($60 a month) or temporarily suspend the massages ($80 a month), or even cut your insurance rates by comparison shopping.

With that money in tow, and a few more steps, you can: realize your dreams, get out of debt, and increase your security and net worth. Isn't it worth it?

You can find money to use by listing your typical expenses, in three categories, simple as "ABC":

A...Necessary expenses
B...Expenses you can reduce
C...Expenses you can eliminate.

Next, cut down like you would weed out non-essentials from a weighty backpack.

With your spending load lightened, you can cross over to the "sunny side" of the street where investing is done.

Investing

Do you have time to select the choicest scenic trails, time to map your trek painstakingly, time to explore endlessly, time to savor the scenery? That's leisurely investing.

For the busy investor, however, investing must be as quick, convenient, and functional as jogging. The following techniques are to saving and investing what a 30-minute jog to the corner is to scaling the Himalayas.

You need some basic equipment, of course, similar to buying a well-fitting, suitable pair of walking shoes for your journey. One size does not fit all, in footwear or in finance. However, if you don't have a no-load, low expense index mutual fund for your investment money, it's usually a good idea to get one, just like certain shoes are recommended for walking.

Chances are the above sentence about "index fund," "no-load," and perhaps even, "mutual fund" didn't mean a lot to you. You don't have to know a lot.

Just as you don't have to know that walking burns calories for that to work for you, neither do you have to know a lot about mutual funds for them to earn money for you.

You can skip the next few paragraphs and still earn money by following the steps outlined.

For the hardy few who are still with me, here are some definitions and explanations:

- A mutual fund is a collection of money or shares you can exchange for money. The professionals

- who manage it decide what companies or what to buy shares in and they charge you, the investor, a management fee for doing all that research and buying and selling. It could be in stocks, bonds, options, commodities, or money market shares.
- A mutual fund has the money divided between different assets, as compared to owning just a share or piece of IBM, an individual stock. Many people think that's a good, safe thing; it's often compared to not putting all your eggs in one basket. I suppose the modern version would be not booking all your football team on the same flight, in case the plane goes down.

The good news about stocks and stock market mutual funds is that historically, they are the best investment of all time. Owning some shares in American businesses is what you're doing, and it even beats buying real estate, bonds, gold, c.d.'s....you name it! What fun! Can't you see yourself saying, "Oh, yes, I own some of that company!"?

Is this getting entirely too serious?
Q: Do you know what a cow's favorite investment is?
A: Why, mootual *funds, of course!*

An index mutual fund is even simpler. These funds invest in a representative basket of stocks of an index (a combination of numbers that measure change)-such as the Standard & Poor's 500 Index-and their returns mirror that index. It's a no-brainer way to at least keep pace with the market. Three-quarters of all professional money managers, according to many reputable sources, do not outperform the S&P500 Index* on a regular basis. No-load (a *load* is a sales charge when you buy) index mutual funds make experts of us all.

Only for Over Achievers: The S&P'S 500 follows the market value of 500 stocks relative to the base period 1941-3. The stocks are mainly industrials (firms which produce or distribute goods or services), with 60 transportation and utility companies and 40 financial issues. Those stocks are what are purchased for one kind of index fund. The costs to you, the investor, are so much lower because it cuts out brokers' fees. Since only one-fourth of all the other professional stock-pickers do only slightly better, the odds are definitely good for a bet on index funds.

The odds are even better that the stock mutual funds will make money for you, if you leave it alone for years, so that it can grow.

Is there any risk? Yes.

I saw a cartoon this morning in which a father was trying to convince his young son that it was possible for stocks to go down. The son didn't believe it.

The stock market has lost up to 43% in one year, but there's never been a 20-year period in which it has lost money. The reasoning goes that the longer you leave the money alone, the better your chances are to make money.

How good? How long? Judging by history, and I do mean history, like going back to 1802, Jeffrey Siegel found that stocks outperform bonds (the second best investment) in a one-year period about 60% of the time, 70% of the time for holding periods of 5 years, 80% of the time for holding periods of 10 years, 90% of the time for holding periods of 20 years, and over 99% of the time for holding periods of 30 years. U.S. stocks have posted an average annual return of 10.5% over a 70-year period.

You could leave your money, say $1,000, under your mattress. There, if no one stole it and you didn't forget where you put it, at the end of the year your money would be worth $970…at about a 3% inflation rate, the average. Sometimes inflation, the rise in the price of goods and services, has been as high as double digits, which would eat an even bigger hole in your stash.

In 1998, your $1,000 invested in Vanguard's Index 500 fund would have earned $286.20, at 28.62% gain. If it was in a tax-sheltered investment, you would have had to pay out only a fraction of a percent for management fees.

You could have put that $1,000 in a certificate of deposit and earned $48.80-at about 2 percentage points above inflation. Sometimes, removing every sliver of risk from your finances can be pretty costly. If your money was taxed, you might have been lucky to make anything on your investment.

Someone who invested $1,000 in the S&P 500 in 1926 would have about $1,112,659 today without investing an additional penny.

There's always some risk in any investment. That's why not all your money goes into a stock index fund. How much? Many planners advise subtracting your age from 100 and putting that percentage of your money in stocks (or a stock index fund). Some advise more. In general, the more you can tolerate risk, the higher the percentage of your money can go in stocks, with a higher potential for earning.

In the chapter on "Fine Tuning," read the section on asset allocation for other options.

If you're 50 years old, for example, 100 - 50 (your age) = 50 (% to invest in stocks).

The other 50% would traditionally be allocated to more conservative investments, e.g. EE savings bonds, CD's, money market funds, annuities, Treasury bills, bonds and notes, cash-value life insurance

An index fund is a good foundation for beginning investors. You can roll over tax-sheltered funds into it, or start one with a small initial deposit. Keeping it simple, you could put a smaller amount of cash in a money market mutual fund or if you don't mind sacrificing the higher interest, to an FDIC insured money market account.

Pick up the phone (or get on the Internet) and order a prospectus for an index mutual fund.

Let's say you chose a good one, based on performance and low cost to you, like Vanguard Index 500. You dial 1-800-635-1511, tell the friendly representative what you want, ask any questions, and hang up.

On the Internet on most browsers, you can simply type the name of the mutual fund, e.g., Vanguard in the location box to reach their site. This works with most companies. Simply type the name with no capital letters; the rest of the URL fills in automatically.

(By the way, you computer users have been warned about viruses. Here are two new ones to worry about: The Airline Virus—you're in Dallas, but your data is in Singapore—and the AT&T Virus—every three minutes it tells you what great service you are getting.)

Remember that you want "no-load" funds and low expenses so that your money is working for you, not going for commissions, loads and fees. Also, you want an IRA or some tax shelter, if you can qualify.

Some people recommend investing in an Index fund that spans the total stock market, which provides even more diversity. Some examples are T. Rowe Price Total Market (POMIX) 1-800-541-8803 and Vanguard Total Stock Market (VTSMX) 1-800-871-3879. The chart on page 67 shows other index funds.

At this point, you have spent nothing. You are not obligated to do anything. Relax. This process works with any mutual funds. You don't have any money? Don't worry about it. You will. Follow the steps outlined in the "Simple Steps to Financial Freedom" Checklist below.

Simple Steps To Financial Security Checklist

___ Gather Records:

* Recent pay stub
* Latest tax return
* Most recent bank statement
* Checkbook
* Current credit card bills

___ List expenses.
___ Divide expenses into 3 categories:

* Regular payments you have to make
* Expenses you could reduce
* Expenses you could eliminate

___ Devise a plan so that you spend less than you take in
___ Start an automatic investment plan
___ Start a savings plan for a fund of 3-4 month's income
___ Arrange to buy any necessary insurance
___ Create and post "Goals Poster."

Organizing

(Optional) If you want to make the rest of the steps and your entire financial life easier, organize your files, next. If the prospect is extremely distasteful or even horrifying, see Chapter 11. "The Kindergarten Filing System.") It's like gathering and packing everything you need for your hike or jog. It's easier if you know where you stowed the water bottle.

Take Inventory

Grab your check book, a calculator, and a big pad of paper with a pencil and:

Add up your expenses for last month for:

- Rent or house payment (Include any association fees)
- Food
- Utilities (electricity, water, fuel, telephone)
- Insurance
- Taxes
- Payments
- Any other absolutely "barebones" necessities like transportation expenses.

If last month wasn't typical, use one that was. If you have a money management program like Quicken, you can get a monthly average of expenses:

Add up your income for last month from all regular, dependable sources. The same comments apply about "typical" and "monthly average." No fair including draws on your credit card or similar borrowing to make it through the month.

Subtract one from the other. Hopefully, the larger amount is your income. If not, we need to talk. It's not hopeless, but you need a major overhaul. Your basic expenses and/or your job choice need evaluation. See Chapter 8, "Debt: When Your Outgo Exceeds Your Income."

The strange thing is—trust me on this—that even if all you do is to make the phone call or begin to notice your expenses, a small cog has changed in your psyche machine which operates the complex part of you called "My Finances." You have already embarked on your new life…your journey.

Setting Goals and Priorities

Where do you want to go? Even a neighborhood stroll requires a destination. Younger people often think us "New Lifers" are beyond romance, dancing or dreams. Not true! Make your goals exciting enough that it inspires you to great effort. You will do whatever you have to do.

What does success mean to you? One of my clients wanted to quit her "day job" and enjoy financial success in her new business as an image consultant.

Another wanted no debt and $1,000,000 net worth.

Another wanted to dissolve her sizeable credit card debt, save $15,000 and go to Europe twice a year with a clear conscience. Obviously, your plan will be as unique as your thumb print.

There are certain tried-and-true processes for hiking, e.g., stretching before you start. There are guidelines for financial security, too.

To free up funds for your goals, ones that excite you because you believe in them, try this:

- Work out a plan to live on 70% of your income, less if possible. When I became serious about finances, we began living on 50% of our income, with a few exceptions. The odd aspect of this monetary crash diet, was that we did not often feel deprived. It was substituting ingenuity for spending, using our wits to save and invest. It was, and is, a game in the best sense of the word. You can feel in control and like you're finally doing " right" for yourself. It's probably similar to a victorious runner's high at the end of a race.
- Invest at least 10% of your income.

Tax Shelters

Plan type	Benefits	Eligibility	Maximum Annual Contribution	Contribution Deadline
IRA	Tax-deferred earnings; may be tax-deductible; can postpone taxes on money rolled over from qualified retirement plan or another IRA	Had earned income; under age 70-1/2	100% of compensation, up to $2,000; annual contributions optional	April 15
SEP-IRA	Reduce taxable profits; 100% vested immediately; easy to set up and maintain	All employees, or the self-employed, age 21 or over, doing work in any 3 of last 5 years	15% of compensation, up to $22,500; annual contributions optional	April 15, or deadline for filing federal tax return
SARSEP	Employee-funded; reduce taxable income; 100% vested immediately	See SEP, above; Participation is voluntary, but 50% of those eligible must participate	Salary deferrals limited—15% of compensation, up to $9240; annual contributions optional	Contributions are normally made during calendar year
403(b)	Tax-deferred contributions; earnings tax-deferred; higher contributions than for IRAs	Employees of nonprofit organizations, such as schools and charities	Generally, maximum of 16-2/3 of annual gross salary or $9,500	Contributions are normally made during calendar year
Profit Sharing	Tax-deductible; earnings tax-deferred; flexible deduction	Employees age 21, after 2 years (or after 1 year if vesting schedule used)	15% of compensation, up to $22,500; annual contributions optional	April 15, or deadline for filing federal tax return
Money Purchase Pension	Tax-deductible; earnings tax-deferred; maximum deduction	Employees age 21, after 2 years (or after 1 year if vesting schedule used)	25% of compensation, up to $30,000; annual contributions mandatory	April 15, or deadline for filing federal tax return
401(k)	Tax-deductible; tax-deferred earnings; optional employer contributions; may reduce company's taxable income	Voluntary participation by employees 21 or older after 1 year of service; optional employer contributions	Salary deferrals limited to 15% of compensation, up to $9,240; optional contributions by employer up to $30,000	April 15, or deadline for filing federal tax return; employer deferrals are usually contributed during calendar year

- Pay yourself first. (Does any of this have a familiar ring?)

First, take advantage of any tax shelters you have available to you: IRA's, SEP's, 401-K's, 403-B's, for example. (See "Tax Shelters, page 87.")

One savings rule is that the number of years you must save for retirement while you're still working must equal the number of years you expect to spend in retirement.

If you don't have that much time, say you're fifty five years old and would like to retire at 65 and expect to live until you're 85.

Ideally, you would have started saving at 45. How can you make up for that?

You must double up on both the amount you save and the return, within certain safety limits, on your investment.

Are you paying the boss first? I don't mean Ol' Grouchy Pants or even Uncle Sam. I mean you. Find out what you need to invest to meet your goal, invest it, and live off the rest.

Here are some ways to "double up":

- Live on 75% of your income. (Don't laugh; people do it even on 50%.)
- Put money in a 401(k) where your employer matches your contribution.
- Invest in stock market mutual funds, or individual stocks to get the maximum growth with an acceptable level of risk. Ibbotson Associates showed how $1 invested in 1925 would have grown in five different investment categories. $1 invested in 1925 in Treasury Bills was worth $11.40 at the end of 1992, while the same amount in small stocks rose to $2,279.04.

401 (k) Guide

One of the best ways to save for your retirement is through your company's 401(k) plan.

I have six steps to make the most of your 401 (k) and to secure your financial freedom in retirement.

Step 1. Focus on your goal.

What do you want your retirement dollars to do? If your retirement is at least ten years away, focus on solid growth investments, such as large-cap stocks. Closer to your retirement goal, if you no longer need to take on a lot of risk, don't be afraid to shift more of your investments to bonds or cash.

Step 2. Contribute NOW.

Even if you start by contributing just 1% of your pay, you must make your financial future a priority.

Step 3. Choose investment options wisely.

Let's talk specifics. If you want growth, start with a stock fund that invests in large U.S. companies. Put 75% to 100% in one or two large-cap funds to build the core of your investment.

As you pile more money in your account, you can branch off into riskier funds like small-company stocks or international stocks. When held in small quantities they can add proper diversification over the long term.

Step 4. Think about your plan when you change jobs.

Don't take the cash. Big mistake. You'll have to pay penalties. You'll have to pay income tax. You lose all that compounding of returns. If your previous employer had good investment choices in its plan and you've invested more than $5,000, you can just leave the money where it is.

If your new employer has better investment options, you can roll the money into the new plan. Or if you want to open up even more investment choices, you can roll the money into an IRA account.

Step 5. Try not to borrow from your plan.

If you blow your retirement savings on a new car, it's like landing on the Go to Jail square in Monopoly. Except for extreme circumstances, it's generally a bad idea to take a loan from your plan. You're derailing your savings plan. Even if you pay it back, you actually end up paying tax twice on the money you put back in your account.

Step 6. Keep beneficiary information up to date. Don't waste all that hard work socking away money just to have it go to someone who's no longer a part of your life. Frequently people wind up with deceased parents, friends from college, or ex spouses listed as current beneficiaries.

SOURCE: Sue Stevens, CPA, CFP, MBA, CFA;
Morningstar's financial planning specialist.

While this sounds incredible, it's true. One year out of the 25 though, the stocks did miserably. Over time, the risk diminishes, so the safest bet may be to 'gamble' on the stock market. The risks of being too conservative are insidious.

- Get a job with benefits so you won't have to pay for protection. (Sounds like the Mafia!)
- If you have investments now, evaluate them in terms of diversity and actual gain.

This may require a fee to a financial planner; sometimes it's obvious. If you have only one investment and it has lost money every year, for example, you know a change is in order. It's easier to get older than it is to get wiser, isn't it?

Before you make any changes, find out the tax consequences to you. Consult a tax person. Eventually, you must have a good accountant, one who is your advocate, not Uncle Sam's, to help you evaluate tax strategies.

If you have no investments, or need the diversity, read the prospectus and fill out the form for an index fund. Send them a check, and you're an investor. You're done for the year. You're going to reinvest your gains and dividends and leave the money alone.

There are advantages to having a monthly automatic deposit made to the fund: Your investing is on automatic pilot and this "dollar cost averaging," as it's called, ensures that some of the time you will buy when the cost of the shares is lower.

You may need to choose a no-load low expense ratio, index fund that has a minimum you can meet. If you have any questions, call that 800 number.

What you want is an automatic deduction every month from your bank account. You can always add more if you want. I'm sorry to say that it is often necessary to exceed the conventional 10% to meet your goals, but we "new lifers" are motivated, right?

There's a rule of 72 to figure how long it takes to double your money. Divide the amount of interest or growth rate of your investments into 72. The result is the number of years is takes to double your money.

For example, you have $20,000. You put it in VFINX (That's the ticker symbol or abbreviation for Vanguard 500 Index Fund.) It had an average annualized total return of 17.9% for the ten-year period, which ended May 31, 1999.

You want $1,000,000 by the time you retire. Dividing 17.9 (Round it to 18) into 72, you get 4, the number of years to reach an investment of $40,000, assuming the rate continues.

Not enough? Try it with increased investment, or a slightly higher interest rate. New Lifers can't afford to risk losing money since their investment horizon is shorter than someone just out of school. The higher paying investments are inevitably riskier. If someone tells you different, keep on walking.

However, stock market mutual funds have been doing well. According to Harry Dent's well-reasoned and documented predictions in *The Roaring 2000's*, they should continue for another 6 or 7 years.

Financial calculators built into money management programs can also tell you when you will reach your goal.. Here's an example: if a person invests 10% of their monthly $4000 salary each year to add to that beginning $20,000, Quicken's software figures that in the 20 years until your retirement at 65, if you're 45 now, that money won't buy as much as it does now. They use a predicted inflation rate of 4%, which you can adjust. By age 65, if you never touch that money, you'll have $2,897,869 but it'll buy what $1,087,039 will today. Of course, it's not usually that simple, but it's a basis for planning.

- Create an emergency fund of 3-4 months wages. Many people have only their credit cards to fall back on in a crisis. That's like starting a twenty-mile walk barefoot, in winter, in Colorado, at a 13,000-foot altitude, with no equipment.

  Census reports found that even well off Americans are living dangerously close to financial instability. 6.5% of those with $68,700 or more a year income had difficulty meeting basic needs ; an estimated 55% to 60% of households carry some credit card debt, says Stephen Brobeck, executive director of the Consumer Federation of America. Interest payments and fees can eat you alive (financially) with a terrible efficiency a grizzly would envy.

- Put your savings in a money market mutual fund that pays the highest interest. Ask if it's insured. Some accounts have FDIC insurance (federal agency guarantees, within limits, funds on deposit

in member banks). If they're lower in interest paid, you decide if it's worth it to you.
- Arrange to buy any necessary insurance. A "bare-bones" plan is:

    disability insurance (to make sure you're covered if you can't work and need that income to live); *health insurance* for medical emergencies; *life insurance*...if you have dependents. (Make sure you're not covered at work and buy term insurance. There are times for cash value life insurance; this is not one of them.) Some people recommend buying term insurance and changing companies every 4 years, taking advantage of lower cost introductory rates. Remember "dependents" are not just children. A business partner can be dependent on you staying alive, too. So can an aging parent.
    Can you say "convertible" and "renewable"? Use these key words when talking to your agent about term insurance. They'll explain what their company offers. It basically means that you can continue to get the insurance (renewable). If you should ever want to (for estate planning or other life passages) you can change (convertible) the term insurance to cash value insurance. Term is renting; cash value is owning.
    property protection (car, house, renter personal possession).
    Special needs (e.g., for your business, or liability) An "umbrella." Liability policy is one example.

- Pay 20% of your income on any outstanding debts. See Chapter 8, Debt: "When Your Outgo Exceeds Your Income" for more detail on debt reduction.
- Decide what you want financially Use very specific money terms. State the end result. Don't stint; this will keep you going when the hills get steep on your path.
    Example: "I am debt-free for everything except my mortgage." or "I have $12,000 (3 months wages) in a savings-type account."
    To say "I want to be financially responsible." is a too general statement, ...although it is a great concept.
- Put Your Goals In Writing!
    Post them prominently. Add pictures that symbolize those goals for you. Enlist a fiscally responsible person to encourage and support you.

Summary—Chapter 5
New Lifers

- *You have a destination that excites you; you really want to go there, your Financial Goals.*
- *You even have full-color photos of it on your wall, your Poster of Financial Goals.*
- *You've gathered, accounted for and organized your equipment, acquiring any needed item, such as sturdy shoes; your Inventory, your Plan to Reduce Spending, and any new savings or investment accounts.*
- *You have a map, so you know how to get there, the "Simple Steps To Financial Security."*
- *You've estimated how long it will take you to go there, a time line.*
- *You're ready to start saving and investing.*
- *You even have a checklist to follow.*

Six

How Not To Ruin Your Children's Lives

Suppose you took your child for a checkup and the doctor finds that he/she is weak and undernourished for their age. Would you provide nutritious meals and more physical activity for them or would you tell them, "I'll exercise and eat for you"?

Of course, that's a silly question. It's obvious how children develop good health and good habits. They strengthen those muscles by using them. They eat the right kinds of food to nourish their bodies. Exercising for them won't work. You can provide nutritious meals, but they have to eat. Their muscles don't benefit from your workouts.

They begin to make wise choices based on the example you set and the learning opportunities you provide. It's that way with money management, too.

The weaker a child or young adult is in money management skills, the more we are tempted to help them out, financially. Watching them get skinned knees and elbows trying to score a goal is difficult for parents, too. Our job sometimes is simply to watch, cheer, and provide coaching…with money or with a ball game.

Unfortunately, gifts of money weaken them further. If you are always hovering above a child or adult like a helicopter, your rotors turning anxiously, ready to swoop down and rescue them, you are not doing them a favor. Au contraire, you are ruining their lives!

The message you send is that "You are weak and I have to provide for you." Where's the respect and trust in their ability to manage on their own? And where's the guidance and training in money skills?

Although my mother is very frugal, I don't think that example was her greatest contribution to me. It was her complete faith that I could handle any challenge, monetary or otherwise. She did not provide money for me. I was on my own, financially at a very early age.

I had hard times. The confidence and independence I gained were worth it. My grandmother used to say, "What doesn't kill you makes you stronger." Now there's a cheerful thought! (Sure to bolster your spirits in time of stress.) And yes, I got really tired of eating peanut butter. Food wasn't taken for granted at one point. Once I even took a jar of home-canned fruit from my landlady that didn't belong to me. (I confessed, later.)

By now, you know that *the greatest gift* is faith in your children, in their ability to be strong, independent people.

It takes your coaching and loving to help them achieve that potential.

Ideally, children would learn by participating in family planning sessions. They would learn about budgeting, the difference between needs and wants, and expect to be "on their own" at a specified age, e.g., eighteen.

They would learn about interest rates, investments and tax on their earnings. They would learn about loans and what happens if you don't make your monthly payments. Few things are more important to a successful life than managing money.

The experiences we provide with money make the difference. One little boy I know was thrilled to be hired to do a job for "fifty cents an hour." His parents were hesitant, but let him do it. The parents checked on him periodically. At first he was enthusiastic, then they noticed a tear trickling down his cheek. "What's wrong, Joey?," his dad asked with concern. "Well, I've been working for hours," the little guy answered, "and nobody's been around with my fifty centses."

My elementary school students were delighted with a visit to a bank, and loved the demonstration of money magically coming out of the ATM machine. It was difficult to convince them that someone had to deposit money in an account before the magic could work.

These experiences provide an opportunity to learn.

Girls, in particular, need to know that it's OK to be financially astute. They need to know that a portfolio can contain something besides art! Imagine a generation that was educated about credit and the magic of compounding! The Consumer Credit Counselors could ease up a bit.

It is heartbreaking and scary to watch your child learn sometimes.

One of the most difficult decisions a parent has to make is when your child is in distress. You want to protect them and take care of them. Sometimes the greater gift is in letting them learn by withholding funds.

One of the gifts of parenting is encouraging your children's' independence, both for your sake and theirs. A good education can aid in their independence and is another of the greatest gifts.

Parenting! What a joyful, stressful experience it can be!

Two mothers are walking their dogs and you overhear the following conversation:

Mom 1: "What is it with kids, Connie? You give them advice and they don't take it. You give them rules and they want to break them...You try to protect them and they disappear. Our youngest rides her bike so fast, I can't watch! She sees stuff on the Internet I never heard of at her age! So as a parent, what can you do?"

Mom 2: "Your best, El...All you can do is your best."

Source: "For Better Or Worse" comic strip by Lynn Johnston.

Just what is your best? I wish I'd known more when we were raising our kids. We did our best. They both turned out to be fine, independent young men in spite of our well-meaning mistakes.

They're watching you!

The first, most important thing you can do for your children is to get your own financial act together...along with a balanced life.

Not only do you provide a good role model, but you won't become a burden to them. Read this poignant letter to the advice columnist, "Dear Abby":

"Learn to just say no to big-time spenders," reads the heading of this column:

Dear Abby: I am 25 years old and have been happily married for three years. My husband is the man of my dreams. We are both hard working and save most of our earnings to meet future goals.

My problem is his mother and father mismanaged their money terribly. Throughout their lives, no matter how much money they made, they spent more. During the past 30 years, when they overspent on phone bills, dinners out, massages, etc., they would ask for money from her brother. Now it's our turn.

Recently my father-in-law took early retirement because he is in poor health due to years of smoking and poor diet. His entire pension was used to pay off their house and accumulated debts. If they had watched their spending, I believe they would have enough through Social Security and her paycheck to pay their bills-yet they are still spending frivolously, acquiring new debt and asking us for money.

This isn't the first time they have asked and received at inopportune moments when we really needed the money ourselves-such as just before our wedding and at Christmas.

We would all love to spend, spend, spend, but it shouldn't be done unless one has the means. I want to be a fair person, but now every time I think of my in-laws I fear they are going to one day wipe us out. How can I prevent it?

...Drowning in their Debt

Dear Drowning: Enough is enough. Your in-laws may need some counseling in prudent financial management. If that is not an option, volumes have been written on the subject.

Saying no won't be easy, but it's important that you draw the line now!"

Saying no, lovingly, is necessary. It also applies to children.

How Millionaires Do It

Stanley and Danko have been studying the wealthy in this country for 20 years. Using their two decades' worth of surveys, interviews, and data they have compiled a detailed picture of who the rich are and how they live.

They reject the big-spending life styles glamorized by the media. Those flashy millionaires actually represent only a tiny minority of America's rich.

In *The Millionaire Next Door*, data collected shows that those receiving gifts and financial help are actually being weakened financially and emotionally. The real tragedy is the helplessness of those who come to depend on what the authors have called "economic outpatient care."

Give This

One of the ways the millionaires do help their children is funding a good education. Research still shows that on the average the higher the level of education, the greater a person's earning potential.

Since college costs and student loan defaults are rising, the kids will probably need to work, too, but be prepared to share the load. Let them see you planning for the cost of a college education.

You can also use education calculators like the one provided on the Internet at Cunamutual.com/realwrld/educcalc.htm

According to the College Board, average college costs in 1996-97 were $7,142 annually for a public college or university and $18,357 annually for a private school. The rate of inflation of tuition and fees for 1996-7 was approximately 6%. You can use a factor of 10% (The average rate of return of the S & P 500 for a twenty year period.) for investment growth if you are invested in stocks or stock market mutual funds.

If your child is in Sixth Grade, for example, a four-year public school college education is projected to cost $45,533. If you start investing $310 a month, earning 10% average yearly, you have a good chance of covering those college costs.

So what is a parent to do, besides saving for a college education?

Children need us, not our money

Love them, but don't give them everything. It's almost a form of neglect or abuse. This sad little story is burned into my memory.

A woman I knew well gave her son everything money could buy. She loved him and it was her way of making up for her lack of time with him.

Millionaire's Rules for Affluent Parents and Productive Children

- No matter how wealthy you are, teach your children discipline and frugality.
- Assure that your children won't realize you're affluent until after they have established mature, disciplined, and adult lifestyles and professions.
- Never give cash or other significant gifts to your adult children because of their high-pressure negotiations with you.
- Stay out of your adult children's' family matters.
- Don't try to compete with your children.
- Emphasize your children's' achievements, no matter how small, not their or your symbols of success.
- Tell your children that there are a lot of things more valuable than money.
- Your children will adhere to the rules if you do. Actions speak louder than words, for sure, for sure.

He became increasingly rebellious, until one night she was called from the county jail; her teenage son had been arrested on theft and drug charges.

When she went to pick him up, she was in tears. "How could you do this, after all I've done for you?" she challenged.

He turned his back on her, saying, bitterly, "You didn't even care enough about me to make me do what's right."

As children grow and seek independence, they become masters at wearing down parents in an attempt to turn every no into a yes.

(Ask me how I know. It took me a while to figure out that our teenagers seemed to approach me with a challenging request the minute their dad left the vicinity.)

Some ways to stand your ground without making enemies of your kids include these suggestions:

- Don't be pressured into giving an instant answer.
- Acknowledge their feelings.
- Present a united front.
- Say yes at least occasionally.

An unknown author wrote:

"Someday I will tell them...
Someday when my children are old enough to understand the logic that motivates a parent, I will tell them;
...I loved you enough to insist that you save your money and buy a bike for yourself even though we could afford to buy one for you.
...I loved you enough to make you take a Milky Way back to the store (with a bite out of it) and tell the clerk, 'I stole this yesterday and want to pay for it....

...I loved you enough to let you assume the responsibility for your actions, even when the penalties were so harsh they almost broke my heart.
...But most of all I loved you enough to say 'no' when I knew you would hate me for it. Those were the most difficult battles of all. I am glad I won them, because in the end you won, too."

Source: *Kids and Money*, by Jayne A Pearl

"When my son Ryan saw a basketball jersey on sale for $28, marked down from $35, he told me, 'We'll save $7 if we buy this now.'

He looked at me quizzically when I responded, 'We'll save $28 if we don't buy it at all.'"

Beginning Money Management

To learn about money, kids first need to have some. Your child is ready for an allowance around age five or six, or when he becomes aware of the relationship between money and shopping; can differentiate coins, can add and subtract; has spending opportunities; and ask you to buy him things.

At the end of the chapter is an "Allowance Guide" for parents to use.

Resist sheltering children from mistakes. Lawrence Kutner, author of five parenting books, including *Making Sense of Your Teenager* gives this example:

"To help my teenager learn how to manage money, I helped him get a checking account. Although I cautioned him about the consequences, he didn't bother to keep a running balance of his account. Lax accounting caught up with him when he wrote a bad check for $10 to a friend. His bank charged him a $20 penalty, and he had to pay the $25 penalty his friend's bank charged-in addition to the $10 he originally owed.

To work off the debt, he did heavy work around neighbor's houses. The natural consequences of his mistake were a far more powerful lesson than any lecture I could have given."

Children and Teens: The Financial Fast Track

Most Olympic stars and professional athletes began early. When we lived in a ski area, Steamboat Springs, I loved watching the 3-year-old ski bunnies playing with the ski instructors as I rode up the chair lift. They were fearless flyers down the ski slopes, those future Olympians.

Their training starts early. If you want to be good at something, an early start helps. Why should learning about money be different?

I want to see more financial education in our public schools, but there *are* ways parents (and grandparents) can help kids learn about money, save for college and even begin to build a large retirement fund.

Several mutual funds help kids learn about money, but Stein Roe & Farnham's Young Investor Fund is leading the way in helping kids of junior- and senior-high-school age develop financial literacy.

The cornerstone of its efforts is a growth stock mutual fund with investments in McDonald's, Disney, Nike, Coca-Cola, Toys "R" Us, and other companies kids see everyday. The average shareholder is nine years old and 85 percent of shareholders invest every month.

Stein Roe & Farnham also provide a wealth of materials to educate the budding investor. You can download an application and prospectus at steinroe.com or obtain information by calling 800-338-2550, for your budding millionaire...or "thousandaire."

Jim Jorgensen, radio talk show host, interviewed Katie, a 14-year-old investor from Illinois, who said, "My mom ...can't believe the money I'm making." Another investor in the fund, 12-year-old Chris from Massachusetts, told the audience, "I first had my money in a bank account and I didn't make much money, so my mom and dad said to invest in mutual funds. So far I've made $400. It's much better than having my money in a piggy bank."

True Tales

Jorgensen, in *Money Lessons for a Lifetime*, reports that both Time Magazine (January 27, 1997) and U.S.A. Today (January 17, 1997) published data that if you invested $10,000 on December 31, 1986, in the S&P 500, you would have $41,935 on December 31, 1996.

If you start at age 20, taking it one day at a time, and saving a mere $2.74 a day, $1,000 a year; invest it in stock mutual funds, and you could have the money you'll need to get by in retirement. That's the kind of fairy tale you can believe in. Children and teenagers need to hear that kind of story.

Here are others:

Ed Blitz in a *Kids & Money* newspaper column writes about Sammy and Daniel, both 16 years old, who have created a computer business based in San Diego called "ComputekSD." They sell custom-built and pre-built computers. They started the business by each contributing $250, earned through small computer repair jobs and Web page design. They can charge less than major retailers can because their expenses are low. Two percent of all profits go to the Make a Wish Foundation. Does their school work suffer?

I'd say "NO!" considering that their G.P.A.'s are 4.17 and 3.67 respectively.

Young Investors Make Profits, opens Corrie Anders' story in the San Francisco Examiner. "Maria and Rory Stevens don't consider themselves real estate magnates just yet. They're more like-well, tycoons in training

"The partners have parlayed a $3,000 stake into an $8,000 bank account and another $40,000 worth of real estate-backed assets that include a 36-foot sail boat, a tavern and three residential properties.

"That's an enviable portfolio, considering that they started their investing career only three years ago! It's even more remarkable when you consider that Maria is a 10-year-old fifth-grader and her brother, Rory, a 13-year-old eighth-grader.

"They are an object lesson for adults and children alike. You're never too young to learn about the investment business…"

Maria, who is into basketball, roller-skating and cartoon sketching candidly admits that the note business (Wall Street Brokers, Inc. founded by their father, Larry Stevens) can be boring at times. Rory, who has been in several school plays, said he wants to become either an actor or novelist. But he said he would stay in the investing business if his other ambitions don't pan out.

> *When "Fireball" Buffett was just eight years old, he began reading books about the stock market, some left around the house by his father. At the grand age of eleven, Buffett began buying stocks in a small way and found his opinions about them were better than others."*
>
> *Warren Buffett: The Good Guy of Wall Street*
> by Andrew Kilpatrick

"Fireball" went from delivering papers to earning money to owning some newspaper businesses; he's now one of the wealthiest men in the world.

Judging by the enthusiastic participation of my students in Newspapers In Education stock-picking contests and a Mini-Society unit where they formed their own classroom country and started their own businesses, children and teens are ready, willing and able to take action in the world of finance.

Young people can earn real money with their own real business. One of my Sixth Grade students (a girl) had a booming graphic arts business, another seized every opportunity to ply his craft of drawing cartoons into cash.

You can share the following with your son or daughter if they show signs of interest:

Steps for Young Entrepreneurs:

First, you need to choose what kind of company you'd like to start. Some examples are computer graphics, pet photography, a lawn-mowing, baby-sitting or pet-sitting business. Plan how you will do it.

Second, get your parents' permission. Tell them exactly what you want to do. They may even have some good ideas.

Third, think of a way to make your company stand out. You need a really cool name and a good or special product. For example, why sell lemonade like everyone else if you can add food coloring and offer a rainbow of colored lemonades?

Fourth, advertise. Distributing flyers is usually very effective. You can even offer a discount at first to encourage interest.

Fifth, make a budget. Show any costs. Determine your prices. See if you would make enough money to justify the effort. Earn or arrange for money to start.

Sixth, make sure you and your product make a good impression. You want people to come back again and to tell others about your business.

Ben Franklin's Way

Children and teens are learning lessons from adults every day, through watching what they do. Sometimes, that's a good thing.

If they hear an adult say, "You don't really need that." In reference to the latest Game Boy or trendy toy, you can bet they notice when the adults "needs" a new stereo component, outfit or exercise gimmick that gathers dust in the corner of the closet.

When Benjamin Franklin wanted to introduce street lighting to the people of colonial Philadelphia, he did not lobby politicians. He did not publish materials. He did not argue with those who disagreed with him. Instead, he simply hung a brilliant lantern on a long bracket in front of his own house.

Every evening, as dusk approached, he faithfully lit the wick. People out in the dark night could see Franklin's streetlight from blocks away and were grateful to walk in its friendly glow.

Soon Franklin's neighbors started putting lanterns on brackets in front of their own homes, and it wasn't long before the entire city was illuminated each night with street lamps.

This is pretty much the way we influence young people. It doesn't work to say, "Do as I say, not as I do."

Of course, with children, parents and teachers are responsible for teaching them how to handle lanterns in the first place. (Or in financial terms, how to handle an allowance and other appropriate activities.)

Whether we have children of our own or not, we are touched more than we realize by young people.

Allowance Guide For Parents

- Decide how much to pay. What's right for your child depends on three factors: the child's level of development, what you can afford, and what you expect him to pay for.
- If your child is itching for a raise, tell him to document increases in the things they pay for.
- Don't tie allowance to grades or behavior; don't automatically increase allowance just because they're a year older.
- Help children decide what to save first, and then see what is left over for spending.
- Encourage young kids to set short-term goals-balloons, stickers, or something they can get in a week. Then move to bigger goals that might take two weeks to save for; later, a month.
- Keep goals and progress visible. When a child decides to save up for, say, a $6 Barbie outfit, you can have her cut out a picture of it and tape it to a glass jar so she can see the money accumulate inside.
- For older kids, you may want to pay matching grants to encourage savings.
- As children get older and start handling more of their own expenses, introduce the idea of budgeting, with a clothing allowance in the fall and spring for example.
- Let your children make mistakes. They may decide to blow their savings on something other than the goal.

Summary—Chapter 6
How Not To Ruin Your Children's Lives

- *To help children learn about money, set a good example in your own affairs.*
- *Don't try to shield them from life's "ups and downs." They need to face some adversity to become strong.*
- *Invite them to learn about business.*
- *Encourage them in good financial habits of saving, investing, careful spending and working toward a goal.*

Seven

What About Stocks?

Most people who are serious about improving finances wonder about the wisdom of investing in stocks.

There are two ways to consider: investing in mutual funds that buy stocks or investing in individual stocks and, in a sense, creating your own "mini-mutual fund."

The mutual fund way is more like visiting a foreign country with a guide; the Individual stock way is more like exploring on your own, with all the risk and effort that it entails. You still get to take the trip, but the latter produces more adrenaline. One investor's "rush" is another's "breakdown."

I believe a beginning investor can invest in individual stocks, but you need the "guide books"; it takes more time, study, effort and a certain temperament. There is also more at stake than a ruined vacation.

Let's look at stocks and some guide books for a safe journey.

Stock Picking Success

To be a success with stocks, many people recommend the following:

Buy stocks in companies you know something about. An alternative to that kind of homework is buying non-speculative stock.

Buy blue chip stocks. A blue chip is the common stock of a nationally known company that has a long record of profit growth and dividend payment, a reputation of high quality management, products, and services. Some examples of blue chip stocks are IBM, General Electric, and DuPont.

Buy regularly, e.g., an automatic deduction from your bank account of a fixed amount. It's called dollar cost averaging. The idea behind it is that some of the time, you're buying at the "right" time, when the stock is lower. You can also buy more when you have spare cash. Novel idea, that. Do NOT try to time the market. I'm sure you've heard of the contest with the dart thrower, supposedly a monkey, who picks stock posted on the dartboard vs. the Wall Street pundits.

It's an annual event; the monkey always wins. It's *probably* an Urban Legend.

Start now. There's never a bad time to get your money working for you. You can probably double your money in less than 5 years.

Buy more than one stock, at least 5, in different sectors. Warren Buffet owns some of Coca-Cola, USA Today, Gillette, and Disney. He's the only person in America in finance who made the "richest persons" list for America in recent times.

Hold on to your stock through the inevitable ups and downs. (Yes, stocks can and will, go down.) The only time you should sell is when the reason you bought the stock is no longer true, e.g. you bought stock in Wells Fargo Bank because you wanted in the financial sector and Wells Fargo started selling clothes and went out of banking. Most losers buy when the stock is high, sell when it's low. That's just the opposite of what J.P. Morgan advised when asked the secret of his wealth, he replied, "Buy low, sell high."

Leave all your money working. Reinvest your dividends. Buffet does.

His investment company, Berkshire Hathaway Corporation, in 1990-1995 delivered a return of 381 percent, compared with 115 percent for the Standard & Poor's 500 stock index. It does attest to his success using the principles I've described. Since most people I know do not have that impressive record, I defer to Warren about stocks. He even admires companies who don't pay dividends, saying there are more lucrative uses of company profits.

Have part of your portfolio in something besides stock or stock mutual funds, even if it's just a super aggressive 5 percent that you put elsewhere. It's called asset allocation and some studies have found that it accounts for 94 percent of your future gains. There is an easy rule of thumb to use: You simply put at least 100 minus your age in stock mutual funds. You need 3-6 months of living expenses in cash (You could put it in a money market mutual fund.) Other possibilities: income-producing real estate, bonds, annuities, CD's.

The more aggressive you want to be, the more you put in stocks or stock (equity) mutual funds

Do NOT go in for "day trading," purchase and sale of a position in securities in the same day. (See Chapter 9, "The Dirty Dozen of Finance.") That's the opposite of holding your stocks and letting them grow.

Investing in individual stocks tends to take more time and generally can involve more risk than investing in mutual funds, but the rewards are potentially greater if you pick the right stocks

"This baby is a cinch to go up!" doesn't count, no matter what your coffee buddy says. Stock picking can't be reduced to a simple formula that guarantees success if you follow it like a recipe.

Focus and Select Funds

One of the criticisms of mutual funds is that they are *too* diversified. The problem with this is that some of the investments, bonds, money markets or a struggling segment of the market drag your gains down.

To offset this, mutual fund managers offer select groups of stocks for a particular industry. Let's say that you really believe that Health Care is a winner for the new millennium, with all the aging Baby Boomers who are living longer and needing those services. An individual stock picker might decide to buy a piece of a company (which is what you're doing when you buy stock) specializing in assisted living for seniors. A mutual fund fan would invest in a Health Care Select Fund.

Focus funds are more like a "mini-mutual fund" with less stocks than the typical fund, but in different industries.

Mutual funds are labeled to show what kind of fund they are, e.g., Vanguard Select Health Care or Marsico Focus Fund.

Common Elements

Here's a summary of the common elements, which you can use to help develop your own stock-picking strategy:

Make sure you adopt a disciplined investment approach, with well-articulated philosophy and investment rules that reflect and refine your philosophy.

Make sure you understand the firm you are investing in-its business and what drives its earnings and revenues, the market in which it is operating, and its prospects.

Seek stocks with reasonable value: low price-earnings, price-to-sales, price-to-book, high yield if you are value-focused; low price-earnings relative to growth if you are growth-focused.

Seek stocks with consistent growth-that is, consistent growth in earnings, dividends, and sales.

Invest in firms with strong financial positions: current assets twice current liabilities and low debt-equity ratios.

Try to find firms that operate in a unique niche, with little competitive pressure.

Small-capitalization stocks offer growth potential and may be overlooked-and undervalued-by Wall Street.

Value investing is well suited for reasonably sound, larger-capitalization stocks.

Growth investing should be tempered with some value investing rules.

Adopt a long-term outlook, ignore market "predictions," and concentrate on the fundamental condition of a firm rather than short-term temporary developments.

How Do the Experts Do It?

There are probably as many "formulas" for successful stock-picking as there are strategies for picking a winning horse at the track. Some of them are as scientific as using the jockey's colors to guide your choice.

To give a glimpse into the principles that guide some of the most successful, here are some comments on three illustrious stock pickers: Warren Buffett, William O'Neil, and Peter Lynch:

Maria Crawford Scott is editor of the AAII Journal. (American Association of Individual Investors) She writes about:

The Warren Buffett Approach

Philosophy and style: Investment in stocks based on their intrinsic value, where value is measured by the ability to generate earnings and dividends over the years.

Buffett targets successful businesses-those with expanding intrinsic values, which he seeks to buy at a price that makes economic sense, defined as earning an annual rate of return of at least 15 percent for at least 5 or 10 years.

Universe of stocks: No limitation on stock size, but analysis requires that the company have been in existence for a considerable period.

Criteria for initial consideration: Consumer monopolies, selling products in which there is no effective competitor, either due to a patent or brand name or similar intangible that makes the product unique.

In addition, he prefers companies that are in businesses that are relatively easy to understand and analyze, and that have the ability to adjust their prices for inflation.

Other factors:

- A strong upward trend in earnings
- Conservative financing
- A consistently high return on shareholder's equity
- A high level of retained earnings
- Low level of spending needed to maintain current operations
- Profitable use of retained earnings
- Stock monitoring and when to sell
- Does not favor diversification; prefers investment in a small number of companies that an investor can know and understand extensively.
- Favors holding for the long term as long as the company remains "excellent"-it is consistently

growing and has quality management that operates for the benefit of shareholders.
- Sell if those circumstances change, or if an alternative investment offers a better return.

Source: *AAII Journal,* November 1998, Volume XX. 10

Buffettology, co-written by Buffett's ex-daughter-in-law, Mary, even tells you which keys to push on a financial calculator to emulate Warren's formulas. It is an education for most just to read it.

There is a web site, BuffettWatch, for those who want to shadow his moves.

You can buy stock in his investment company, Berkshire Hathaway, selling at around $70,000 per individual Class A share! (No, that's not a typo. It's really seventy thousand for one share. I could have bought it a few years ago for a mere $20,000 a share.) Warren himself says his stock is not a good investment...too expensive. He also has probably not revealed all his "secrets" to his adoring public.

This sketch does not even scratch the surface of his approach.

The William O'Neill Approach Founder of "Investors Daily," William O'Neil, on the other hand, has written a classic book, *How to Make Money in Stocks*. He shares his approach with us:

"Here's a sneak preview of C-A-N S-L-I-M.

C = Current Quarterly Earnings Per Share: How Much Is Enough?

A = Annual Earnings Increases: Look for Meaningful Growth.

N = New Products. New Management. New Highs: Buying at the right time.

S = Supply and Demand: Small Capitalization Plus Volume Demand.
L = Leader or Laggard: Which is Your Stock?
I = Institutional Sponsorship: A Little Goes a Long Way.
M = Market Direction: How to Determine It?"

The Peter Lynch Approach Peter Lynch, another highly respected authority who managed the top ranked Fidelity Magellan Fund, until his retirement in 1990, gives "Twenty Golden Rules" at the end of his best seller, *Beating the Street*. He agrees with many of Buffett's practices. I particularly agree with his concluding Rules (18 and 20):

"If you don't study any companies you have the same chance of success buying stocks as you do in a poker game if you bet without looking at your cards...."

"In the long run, a portfolio of well-chosen stocks will always outperform a portfolio of bonds or a money-market account. In the long run, a portfolio of poorly chosen stocks won't outperform the money left under the mattress."

The DOW Dividend Approach

This is a simple way to intelligently select your own stocks. There are vastly simpler ways to stupidly select stocks, as the Random Portfolio and the Intoxicated Investor Portfolio, or the Dartboard Approach.

A word of caution: all the information presented in this chapter is just a start. Please, please don't skip the important step of reading the inexpensive paperbacks, which explore these issues and these methods in greater depth.

The Dow Dividend strategy was popularized by Michael O'Higgins, a former top money manager and current champion of the individual investor. The approach is shockingly simple and wildly effective, by most accounts.

In order to calculate your own version of the Dow Dividend, you'll need to know three important numbers: the stock price, it's current dividend and it's dividend yield, which is simply the dividend divided by the stock price. All you do is rank the list of 30 stocks from highest yield to lowest, and voila, you have accomplished your research. (In the event of a tie, simply use the stock with the lowest price for share.)

There are three main variations of the Dow Dividend Approach:

The High Yield 10 Buy top ten yielding stocks from the list (in equal dollar amounts, not equal share amounts) and hold them for one year. After the year is up, update your statistics, sell any of your stocks not still on the top ten list, and replace them with the new highest yielders. Simple enough?

Beating the Dow Start with the same ten stocks used for the High Yield 10, but buy only the five least expensive of the ten. Read Michael O'Higgins *Beating the Dow* and visit cassandrasrevenge.com for more information on this approach.

The Foolish Four This approach includes the four cheapest of the high-yield stocks instead of five, with one qualifier. If the lowest-priced stock of the High Yield 10 also has the highest dividend yield in the group, skip it and buy the next four stocks. Read the *Motley Fool* column or visit their web site fool.com for more on this approach. It's also a great spot for information on stock-picking in general and on investment clubs.

Broker or Not?

What about paying a really good broker or financial planner? Yes, that can work. I've heard two or three success stories out of about ten horror stories. Two of the horror stories we experienced personally. That is obviously not a scientific observation.

No one cares about your money more than you do. You have to maintain a watchful attitude when someone else is handling your money. Even if he/she is a patron saint of finance, take some responsibility. What if they leave? Die? Retire? Sell to gain commissions rather than to make you money?

If you have found your financial wizard, make sure you ask questions and are not in a constant "sleep mode." Evaluate the results of their money handling on a regular basis, perhaps once a year. Maintain a balanced love-hate relationship. And keep reading.

Are You Ready for Stocks?

If you're seriously considering stock-picking on your own, you brave, beginning individual investor, let me ask you:

"How much time, money, and effort are you willing and/or able to expend in choosing stocks?"

"Are you susceptible to selling everything in a panic?"

"Do you feel like having a Prozac shake every time your stocks dip?"

"Are you willing to work to learn a business-like strategy and stick to it?

Stocks can be very rewarding for those who have the stomach, stamina, savvy, time and money for them. Otherwise, it's like Ted Allen says, "Buying a stock is exactly the same thing as going to a casino, only with no cocktail service."

If you're ready for stock-picking on your own, you can get valuable information using Value Line or Standard & Poor's at the library, usually at the Reference Desk. The Internet offers much company information as well. Try these sites:

- Quicken.com
- Snap.com
- stocksite.com/index.ssj
- thestreet.com
- fool.com

DRIPs

Consider companies which have Dividend Reinvestment Plans that do not charge a commission. (DRIP's). Examples (The phone number will put you in touch with the company's DRP officer.):

- Coca-Cola Co. (404) 676-2777
- Colgate-Palmolive Co. (212) 310-2575
- General Electric (800) 786-2543
- Johnson & Johnson (908) 524-3896
- McDonald's Corp (800) 621-7825
- Rubbermaid Inc. (216) 264-6464
- Wm. Wrigley Jr. Co. (800) 824-9681

DRIPS enable you to build a stock portfolio with small investment dollars by investing directly with the company without going through brokers or paying brokerage fees. See a list of hundreds of DRIPs at investorguide.com/DRIPs.

Consider what happened with the Marsico Fund when it first started. It opened at $18.00 per share July. In August, it dropped to $16.50 per share. In October, it had risen to $18.25. By November, it was up to $19.15.

What if we'd sold it in August when it dropped in price, or in October, thinking it wouldn't go much higher? Choose carefully, and then hold on…unless the reason you bought it is no longer true.

Is Stock-Picking For You?

Here are the key questions to ask yourself about stocks as an *investment*, not a gamble:

- Do you have at least $25,000 to invest?
- Do you have long term financial goals? Twenty years before you need to draw on investments for income is an example of a long-term investment horizon.
- Can you take the inevitable rise and fall of the stocks in stride?
- Do you have time for research?

If the answer to all of those questions is "Yes," maybe stocks are for you!

Summary—Chapter 7
Stock-Pickers' Success Plan

- *Balance your life and portfolio-debts handled, budget established and emergency fund filled.*
- *Acquire $25,000 or more for investing purposes.*
- *Evaluate the appropriateness of individual stocks for you. If it's a fit, proceed.*
- *Develop your stock-picking strategy.. Practice with a hypothetical portfolio.*
- *Locate a list of DRIP companies.*
- *Choose 5-8 target companies using your strategy.*
- *Open a brokerage account to purchase your initial stocks (a single share in each company) in these companies, using a discount broker.*
- *Sign up for each company's DRP.*
- *Buy more shares commission free.*
- *Don't sell your shares unless you must.*

Eight

Debt: When Your Outgo Exceeds Your Income

One of the best debt reduction strategies is to *do nothing!* Don't go to garage sales; don't read sale catalogues; don't watch or read advertisements; don't "window shop." After all, how many ceramic cats or plastic flamingos do we need?

The operative word is "need." Everyone needs/wants a few luxuries, but the idea is to be on a strict money diet until the desired weight is reached. Once your "metabolism" has been reset and your new, good habits have been established, you can consume more and not fatten your debt.

Some couples go into debt or require a second income just to support their sports utility vehicle! A census report found that even well-off Americans are living dangerously close to financial instability, even those at the top end of the income spectrum, with annual incomes above $68,700.

Confucius says: *When prosperity comes, don t use all of it.*

Consolidation

Consolidate high interest credit card, auto and student loan debt into a cheaper and potentially tax deductible loan using the equity in your home.

For non-homeowners, the best way to consolidate your debt is to transfer your higher rate credit card balances to a lower rate card. Getsmartinc.com on the Internet helps you shop for the best rates on either.

As a rule, avoid "credit repair" and commercial consolidation services.

Call (800) CCCS for information on non-profit organization Consumer Credit Counseling Services, instead.

The Federal Trade Commission is your best all-round bet on getting satisfactory and accurate information which you can personally put to use. Their Net site address is www.ftc.gov/.

Choose Credit to go to a long list of helpful online documents/publications which you can access. Offerings include: Divorce and Credit; Credit Repair: Self-Help May Be Best and Knee-Deep in Debt. You can also call 1-877-FTC-HELP. "insiderreports.com" offers the scoop on credit bureau myths and credit repair. Another good source is National Foundation for Consumer Credit, 1-800-388-2227 or nfcc.org.

Cutting Expenses And Getting In Shape

Just like quitting an addiction abruptly..."cold turkey"... can be effective, so starting your new, healthier money style can begin at once.

Most people can cut expenses dramatically; most people can increase their earnings. Combine the two and you have a miracle underway, IF you use that "found money" to reduce your debts and increase your investments.

Sounds sort of like eating less and exercising more, doesn't it?

The miracle is that your money begins to work for you! Rich people have known that for ages. The rich spend their money on assets, such as:

- Mutual funds
- Rental real estate
- Stocks (You own a piece of a business.)
- Bonds (IOUs; A business owes you money)
- Businesses that don't require your presence
- Notes (loans to others).

According to *Rich Dad, Poor Dad* author, Robert Kiyosaki, poor people spend all their money just on surviving. Middle class people spend money on liabilities they think of as assets but which actually cost them, e.g. automobiles, boats and homes in some cases. Rich people spend money on assets, which put money *in* their pockets.

His definition of liability is "anything that takes money out of your pocket." An asset is "anything that puts money *into* your pocket."

If you live in the San Diego area, there is a gem of a book to help you with your money "reducing diet" called *San Diego's Deals & Steals* by Sally R. Gary. Email her for a copy sallygary@aol.com.

A friend of mine (Thanks, Tish) gave me a subscription to *Bottom Line/Personal*, ($39 for 1 year to Bottom Line/Personal Subscription Service Center, P.O. Box 50379, Boulder, CO 80323-0379) a periodical that covers finance and thrift from many angles. I've renewed it repeatedly because it improves the quality of our lives, financially and otherwise.

There are other money-saving books and publications out there, like the *Tightwad Gazette* periodical or *The Penny*

Pincher, Mendham, NJ. I'd love to hear from you readers with your favorites.

They offer amazing insights into the fine art of dollar stretching. (See "Avoiding Big Money Blunders" in this chapter.)

If you really want to lose weight or cut down spending, keep a record of every morsel you eat or penny you spend. *(I think licking postage stamps is one calorie.)*

The key word to reducing your outgo of money is "creativity."

John Capozzi of IMC Investments offers an awesome lesson in resourcefulness:

> *He was faced with a huge rock, about five feet in diameter, in the middle of a dirt floor basement he and his wife were remodeling in 1971.*
>
> *Bids ranged from $2,800 (dynamiting) to $2,200 (pneumatic air hammer), which in those days was a lot of money. He was very depressed by these high estimates. The rock had to go, but what was the right way to get rid of it?*

He tells the story this way:

> *Suddenly, I had a thought.*
>
> *I asked my lead digger how long it would take to dig a hole six feet by six feet right next to the rock. He said, "Three hours." At $10 per hour, I gave him the go-ahead.*
>
> *When the hole was completed, we assembled the entire crew and pushed the rock into the hole. It completely vanished at a total cost of $30.*
>
> *The basement was beautifully and functionally finished as planned.*

A friend of mine was faced with divorce and the support of three children. She couldn't afford to pay the house payment; had no job skills and her ex-husband did not come to her rescue. Did she panic? Maybe.

What she *did*, however, was move her family into a rental for half the cost. She rented her mortgaged home for slightly more than the payment

Family and friends helped out while she acquired a teaching degree. Her actions changed a crisis into an opportunity.

Let's brainstorm for a moment on some so-called " fixed expenses" using "possibility thinking" on how even *they* can be reduced. Possibility thinking rules out no idea, no matter how outrageous, with the idea that the gold can be mined out of the pile of dirt, later.

Taxes Take taxes (*Take them*, Please…), the number one expense for most people:

- You could see your accountant to find out what you could do to reduce your tax bill.
- You could stop paying income taxes.
- You could move to one of the 10 states that don't have income tax.
- You could buy a house or condo, acquiring a tax deduction on interest paid
- You could start your own business and use those deductions.
- You could convince someone else to pay your taxes.
- *Your ideas:*
-
-

Actually the best idea is probably to see your accountant, although I'm not discounting your creative solutions.

I'm a big fan of hiring good professional help when you need it, and Stanley and Danko in *The Millionaire Next Door* report the usually frugal millionaires they interviewed do the same.

Rent or House Payments
- Refinance your mortgage if you can gain from it. (See Chapter 12, "Fine Tuning.")
- Run your own luxurious mansion, renting to friends.
- Become a caretaker on an estate. Recently I read about a couple whom were paid to live on the grounds of a luxurious Rancho Santa Fe, California estate. The owner was there only a fraction of the time.
- *Your turn:*
-
-

Electricity
- Try one of the new "green power" utilities who are currently subsidized by the federal government, like Commonwealth;(Call 1-800-CALIFORNIA or visit the World Wide Web at http://www.powersavers.com. You reduce your bill and do something good for the environment, too, since their power source is geothermal. Isn't that on a par with fat-free brownies? Another choice is the wind-powered Green Mountain Energy, 1-888-246-6730 or greenmountain.com.

Insurance
- Compare six companies' rates to get the best deal. Good bets for cheaper auto insurance, if you can meet their requirements, are: GEICO (800-861-8380 or geico.com; USAA (for the military com-

munity), usaa.com; 20th Century (800-211-7283); Wawanesa (800-640-2920). According to a report released by Standard & Poor's, State Farm Group had the largest volume of premiums in 1997-1998, but had a higher percentage of "justified complaints" (12.2percent) than Wawanesa (4-5percent) (Source: California Department of Insurance.).
I found this and many other statistics on insurance companies at insure.com on the Internet.
- You can lower your rates with discounts with your existing company. Allstate offers safe driving, multiple insurance, antilock brakes, defensive driving class and many other discounts, for example. Ask your agent how you can reduce your bill. Ours spent hours with us lowering our costs $300 a year.
- Make sure, with any insurance, that A.M. Best, Moody's Investors Service or Standard & Poor's rates the company "excellent" or better. You want the company where you buy your policy to be around when you need it.
- In addition, find out what you need to know about the protection. *Consumer Reports* offers concise explanations online (consumerreports.org), or in their magazine, which you can read at the library. I consider my online subscription, at $2.95 a month, money well-spent (consumerreports.com).
- Insurance agents are another good source, particularly when evaluating a rival policy. They are actually trained to know the competition's strong and weak points, in many cases. Of course, check the info out with another source.

Telephone
- Compare. This is a highly competitive market. I usually refer to our last month's bill from my current company and ask a rival what they would charge for the same services. Join one of the many long-distance calling plans offered by AT&T, Sprint, MCI and other carriers. Long distance rates are rising fast.

Water
- Adjust your automatic sprinklers to save water. When we lived on two acres, we could have qualified for a discount based on the quantity of water used and whether or not we sold any produce. The sale of even one box of fruit met their requirements!

Real Estate Taxes
- Sometimes you can qualify for a reduction, if your property has been dropping in market value, for example. Contact your county tax office.

Income Taxes
- Withholding too much in tax from your paycheck is like giving the IRS an interest-free loan. Consult your company's benefits department or your tax preparer to help you calculate the correct amount.

Credit Cards
- Call card companies and ask them to lower interest rates on cards you already have. Use one of those card offers crowding your mailbox as leverage.

    Kerry Clark, manager of branch services at Consumer Credit Counseling Service of Greater Atlanta did just that. The interest rate on his card was lowered by 5 percent for a year.

It can be fun, outwitting the specter of so-called Fixed Expenses. Of course, I'm an advocate of the "have your cake and eat it, too" philosophy. Why can't you eat half the cake and save some (to have)? I always wondered.

I've also wondered why "the buck stops here" doesn't mean more money in your pocket instead of more responsibility.

If you don't know that it can't be done, it's lots easier to do it. Personally, I'd rather save money on taxes and insurance, if I can do it safely, than on say, entertainment and travel. How about you?

Also, avoid shopping in establishments where you see any of these signs:

Why go elsewhere to be cheated when you can come here?

Or a loan company:

Ask about our plans for owning your home.

Or ye olde country shoppes that advertise:

We buy junk and sell antiques.

Credit as A Friend

Debt *used to be* a four-letter word. According to an article "Debt Management" on the SmartMoney.com Internet site, one reason debt has become more palatable is that the prime rate has fallen from 21.5 percent to 8.5 percent today. At the same time, the stock market has had a seven-year bull run, with the S&P 500 averaging 19.18 percent annual gains since 1992. That has created an easy arbitrage. Borrow at 8 percent, invest at 19 percent and get rich.

"But not everyone is balancing their debts and investments so successfully. In 1997, personal bankruptcy filings were nearly 55 percent higher than they were in 1991....The credit card offers that crowd our mail boxes are too much for some individuals to handle," they conclude.

As one newborn in the hospital nursery says to another, You know what's cool? We re all born with an automatic $5,000 credit limit.
Mick Stevens in U.S.A. Weekend

One of the best in-depth treatments of the subject is in Beth Kobliner's book, *Get A Financial Life*. I will cheerfully refer you to it, as I offer only highlights and very simple actions here.

Other books on debt abound: *10 Minute Guide to Beating Debt,* by Susan Abentrod, and *Credit Card Management*, by Scott Bilker, are two I found on Amazon.com.

All of the following guidelines and suggestions are ideal scenarios and need to fit your individual situation. For example, it is a rule of thumb that no more than 30 percent of your take-home pay should be spent on mortgages or rent. In San Diego, where I live now, you would be reduced to a closet or sharing quarters to meet that criterion in many cases. So, with that in mind, read on.

How Bad Is It?

Your total debt, not including your mortgage, should be less than 20 percent of your annual take-home pay.

Use savings, or allot 20 percent of your take home pay each period, for paying off your highest-rate debt first.

Rarely does it make sense to raid your IRA, 401(k) or other investment to pay off your credit card loan, unless you are 59 ½ or older. Why? You will owe a 10 percent penalty and income taxes on all withdrawals. A Roth IRA account is different; seek expert tax advice before going there.

Transfer debt from high-interest-rate loans to lower-rate loans (refinancing).

No matter how you work it, however, having debt is usually HHH (*Highly Hazardous* to your financial *Health*). Paying off a loan with a 16 percent interest rate, for instance, is in effect paying yourself a 16 percent rate of return, *tax-free*. That's a rate even the most ambitious broker can advertise happily.

That's why it is good finance to get rid of debt before you get too creative with investing. The debt undermines what you make.

Financial Windfall

Suppose you receive an inheritance, hit it big at the slot machines, or win a lottery?

Hire the right financial advisor. According to John Markese, president, American Association of Individual Investors, before hiring a financial advisor:

"Carefully read Part II of the *Securities and Exchange Commission Form ADV,* which must be given to clients. It explains services, fees, investments and the adviser's educational background. Also request Part I of the form, which details legal history. Check the adviser's track record and consistency of performance."

Pay down debt before making investments Start by eliminating your most expensive debts first. The typical steps:

- Get rid of credit card debt first (9-20 percent interest rate).

- Eliminate car loans (usually around 10 percent).
- Pay off home-equity lines of credit (variable rates).
- Then, pay off life insurance loans (about 7.5 percent)
- Last, decide whether you're better off, financially and emotionally, investing the remainder in a stock mutual fund or paying off your home mortgage.

It's even better to build up your savings, so you won't have to turn to a credit card every time an expense pops up. That's like stocking your refrigerator with succulent, juicy, fresh, appetizing fruit and vegetables for times when the hungries hit. So, even if you pay some more interest on your credit card debt, build up 6 months expenses in savings.

If you must borrow, always shop for the lowest interest rates…the low-fat versions. Read the fine print, however. Most people are now aware of low "teaser rates" on credit cards for example, that vanish after a few months, leaving you with heftier charges.

Two good sites on the Internet to compare rates on many kinds of credit are: http://www.bankrate.com and http://www.ramresearch.com. Newspapers and financial magazines also carry rate comparisons. I like the Credit Card Finder on getsmartinc.com.

Confine your search for a charge card to a financial institution that offers credit cards. Investigations by Better Business Bureaus across the country show that advertisements that promise credit cards but that are not directly from credit card issuers, have been limited or misleading in many cases.

Limit your access to credit by carrying only 1 or 2 credit cards. (Make sure you have at least one loan or credit card in your own name if you're married. If you don't, you will have trouble getting credit if you get divorced or if your spouse dies.)

Pay cash or write checks for purchases; use the most painful method for you.

Your goal is to pay the credit card balance off entirely and to not carry a balance from month to month. You may want to transfer your debt to a credit card with a lower rate, adhering to a schedule and a target date to pay it off completely.

While you're getting to that point, take note of the following suggestions:

- Pay your bill the day you get it.
- Pay more than the monthly minimum and resist the "Skip-a-payment offers."
- Use a debit card if you have trouble controlling your spending.
- Don't use your credit card for cash advances. It's very expensive credit.
- Ask your current credit company for a better deal..
- Evaluate "give back" cards carefully, e.g, frequent flyer miles for every dollar you charge. They may offer higher rates for benefits you never use.
- Get the lowest annual fee/interest charge card. (See "Negotiating a Lower Rate," page 149.)
- Before you transfer a balance, check the new card's fine print. Here are some basic questions to ask as you comb through that low-rate credit card offer:

    ❏ How much is the annual percentage rate after the teaser rate expires?
    ❏ Does the teaser rate apply to transferred balances, new purchases or both?

❏ Does that card have an annual fee?
❏ What about late fees and over-the-limit fees?
❏ How long does that enticingly low introductory rate last?
❏ Is there a fee for transferring the balance?
❏ Will you lose the low rate if you miss other payments or significantly increase your total debt?

Source: bankrate.com

Keep in mind that not everyone who gets an offer qualifies for the super-low rate. Also realize that it may only take one slip-up for the super-low rate to disappear. With one late payment, kiss that low rate goodbye. For example, a Platinum MasterCard from Fleet with a 9.99 APR jumps to 21.99 percent after one tardy payment.

Balance Transfers

The new card company may send a notice saying the balance transfer is complete. Be sure to call the old card company and verify this. Write down the name of the person you talked to, the date, the time and what was said.

It's a good idea to make the minimum payment on the old card while waiting for the transfer to take place-which may take anywhere from two to four weeks.

To avoid any mix-ups, experts urge people to wait until the old credit card company sends them a billing statement with a zero balance. If the company doesn't send one, request it.

Next step: cancel the old card. You don't want to stock up on credit cards anymore than you fill the pantry with your favorite candy and cookies when you're trying to slim down. Cut up the old card and mail it to your old company. It's very symbolic, satisfying and final.

Consumer experts also urge people who transfer balances to a low-rate card to stay with it a year or more. You need to build a credit history. Too many inquiries on your credit report can make you look shaky.

Loans

Do you have student loans? You can refinance to a lower rate or consolidate your loans. Call 800-4FED-AID to get facts.

Prepay loans faster than your current payment schedule requires if you can.

Get a deferment if you need to put off payment in an emergency. Contact the institution that's handling your loans to learn more about deferments.

By extending the number of years over which you pay back your student loans, you can reduce monthly student loan payments and free up some cash to pay off your credit cards.

Car Loans

Before you visit a car dealership or start shopping for that vehicle, consider the finances from several angles.

Know what you want? Check it out for insurance costs (your agent), repair records (*Consumer Reports*) and get an idea of the current auto loan rates from a couple of banks and a credit union if you belong to one.

Once you find the car you want, negotiate an exact price for a car with the dealer before you discuss the financing he has to offer. You can check the value of your old car at kbb.com (*Kelley Blue Book* prices) or at the library.

If you own a home, consider taking out a home equity line in order to pay off your high-rate debt. But plan to pay off your home equity line as fast as you would have paid off the loans you're refinancing.

Home Equity Loans

If you own a home, you're usually allowed to borrow about 80 percent of your home's value *minus* the balance on your mortgage. It offers a lower interest rate than credit cards and a tax break. For this reason, taking out a home equity loan to pay off other higher-rate debt makes sense.

The chief drawback of home equity loans is that borrowers can lose their homes if they can't make their payments. The home equity loan is typically a fixed rate.

This is different from Home Equity Lines of Credit, which are similar to credit cards.

Both of them, however, are dangerous as a credit card substitute. Remember, if for any reason you can't make your payments, that the lender will be allowed to take your home.

Be diligent about paying off the home equity loans as quickly as you would have paid off the loans you're refinancing. Otherwise, it becomes just another credit card with extra hazards.

Don't forget to figure in the fees the lenders charge when granting home equity loans and lines of credit.

Watch out for variable interest rates that come with a home equity line and ask the loan officer just how much the rate can rise.

Before you apply for a major loan, you can check your credit report thoroughly for errors by sending a written request to Experian (formerly TRW). Call 888-397-3742 for details or order online at experian.com. It is free, one per year.

If you find a mistake, write to the agency right away. They're required to send a corrected version of the report to any lender at your request.

Stay away from any company that claims to repair credit ratings. Don't waste your money. Lenders usually look at your behavior in the last 2 years when evaluating your creditworthiness. Most negative information will be deleted after 7 years.

Deep Trouble

If you're drowning in debt:

- Contact your lenders directly and explain your financial situation. Often they'll work with you to come up with a more flexible repayment schedule. Sometimes, they'll even forgive a portion of the debt. I still remember my mother negotiating to retire the medical and custodial care debts that piled up during my grandmother's last years. The institutions were more than fair.
- Bankruptcy is an option, but filing for it haunts your employment and credit records, thus hurting your prospects for years to come.
- CCCS offices (Consumer Credit Counseling Service) offer free or low-cost. To locate an office near you, call 800-388-2227. The key word is "non-profit" organization. The Federal Trade Commission offers much good, unbiased debt management advice. Some colleges and credit unions offer such services.

Http://mmintl.org/ is a site on the Internet that offers free debt counseling. Many others do, as well.

Except for funds held in a Roth IRA account for more than five years or the original contributions in a Roth IRA, you will owe a 10 percent penalty and income taxes on any withdrawals from 401(k), 403(b) and regular IRAs or tax sheltered annuities, so withdrawing from those accounts to pay off debt is a bad move.

Garnishment

If you do not pay your legal debts, your creditors can sue you and obtain a judgement against you. The judgement may entitle them to garnish your wages. In other words, your employer could be legally required to send a portion of your wages to your creditors. There are limits to how much of your pay can be garnished. *Source: Consumer Credit Protection Act, 1968.*

Most states have similar laws. Check to determine local regulations. If an employee's credit performance becomes so improper that the employer is overloaded with garnishment claims, the employer could dismiss them.

In other words, you can be fired, jailed, lose your worldly goods and/or your credit cards if you get too far out of line with debt.

If you have reached this embarrassing and financially devastating point, RUN to seek the help mentioned above.

Mortgages

Buying a home is probably the best debt you can have. It has tax advantages, emotional value and impact on your lifestyle. However, view your home carefully. It is not always an asset.

Anyone who has paid on a mortgage, home repairs, property taxes, and home owners' insurance is well aware that a home can take money out of your pocket. Unfortunately, a home doesn't always increase in value, either. It is a popular myth that they always do.

Real estate, as an investment, can be highly lucrative. It requires some knowledge and research to make it pay off, however. I love real estate, but I think there are many misconceptions about home-buying.

Anyway, a mortgage for your home or rental property is a major investment that deserves devoted attention to the following:

- Before you go hunting for a home of your own, get pre-qualified for a mortgage (by your bank or your agent's real estate company). This gives you an idea of how large a mortgage you can afford.
- Get as much information about the home you want to purchase as possible. Is it a "good buy"? How are the neighborhood schools? Is it over-priced for the neighborhood? Is the house defective in any way? There are books on home buying. You can consult experienced home buyers.
- Shop for a mortgage. The Federal Reserve Board offers a truly helpful site on the Internet for mortgage shoppers. They offer explanations and a Mortgage Shopping Worksheet. If you ask the questions they list, I guarantee you will get more respect from a broker, even if you're not positive what the questions mean!

To narrow down the lenders by interest rate, check out more nifty sites and newspaper listings for current interest rates offered and other relevant information:

Bank Rate Monitor and HSH are two I've used. On Netscape Navigator, just type in bank rate or hsh and it will fill in the rest of the URL.

Increasing Your Earnings

Suppose you apply the brainstorming method to your own career situation.

Ask yourself, "How can I make more money in my current job?" Sometimes there are clear options to choose. Teachers are on a salary schedule, for example, but they can add to that salary by increasing the number of college credits/ degrees they have or taking on additional duties like mentoring.

You can work smarter, whatever that means in your situation and sometimes have it pay off in cash.

Conventional wisdom says that the more skills/knowledge/degrees you have, the more money and security you will acquire. But we're talking about you and today's world. What would it take to increase *your* earning power?

If the answer, according to you and the people you consult, is to change jobs, to take certain classes, or even to start your own business, I have good news.

The variety and quality of support available, free or low cost, to people in America is inspiring. Here's a sampling:

Free Classes and Workshops Now that computer prices are plummeting and deals abound, I believe you should go online. Don't know enough to even buy a computer? Enlist someone who does or take free classes offered at a community college on choosing and using your first computer.

The Small Business Administration offers a web site <http://gopher.sbaonline.sba.gov/starting/indexbusplans.html> that tutors you in creating a business plan, financing and other matters involved in a small business. SCORE is a volunteer branch of SBA that's invaluable for small business owners.

You can use the Internet:

- As a place for you to search for jobs openings (often called want ads).
- As a place to post your own resume.
- As a place to get some career counseling help
- As a place to do research or find info about fields, occupations, companies, cities, geographical areas, etc.
- As a place to make contacts with people, who can help you get in for an interview at a particular place.
- As a place to conduct business and to advertise.

Author Richard Nelson Bolles, of *What Color Is Your Parachute?* fame, offers a good web site, Bolles' Parachute Picks for Online Job Hunters, for "income increasers."

His entertaining overview covers the use of search engines (to find what you want on the Internet), career counseling and much more. To get to it, type: http://www.jobhuntersbible.com/ in the location box once you've signed on.

Other sites include:

- The Riley Guide <http://www.dbm.com/jobguide>
- JobHunt: A Meta-list of Online Search Resources and Services <http://www.job-hunt.org>
- Job Pointer <http://www.dog-ear.com>.

Which reminds me, did you know the following breeds are now officially recognized by the American Kennel Club?

Poinsetter, a traditional Christmas gift dog, a cross between a flower and a setter; and the NewFound Asset Hound, a cross between a basset hound and Newfoundland, a dog that's good with finances.

Ten Painless Ways to Save

- Put your credit cards somewhere other than your wallet, like a safe deposit box in your bank. The cards are still available if you really need them.
- Make a game of turning off lights, taking shorter showers, turning down thermostats and then seeing how much you save on utility bills.
- Try putting broken mechanical or electronic devices in the basement and doing without them. You may not even miss them.
- Try cooler temperature settings for a wash.
- Substitute potluck dinners with friends or create a "restaurant night at home with special food and decorations, instead of dining out.
- Go over insurance policies to be sure you're paying for protection only against large or disastrous losses.
- Get acquainted with food prices. Then when you see a real sale, you can stock up.
- Turn down your water heater to 115 degrees, or cool the house only to 77 degrees.
- Write this on an index card and post it on your refrigerator: "Want what you have and you'll always have what you want."
- See if you can get the job done with smaller amounts, e.g. toothpaste, shampoo.

from *Live Well on One Income* by *Andy Dappen*

Avoiding Big Money Blunders

- Don't always buy new products.
- Don't buy a used car until a mechanic has checked it out thoroughly.

- Don't overpay for college. Tell your kids at a young age.10 is good... that they'll be partly responsible for tuition; get an employer or the federal government to help pay.
- Don't discard things too soon.
- Don't be a clotheshorse. Buy good quality; buy on sale. Buy washables.
- Don't overspend on the kids. Making kids responsible for their entertainment and toys teaches them the value of money-and keeps extra money in your pocket.

Negotiating a Lower Rate

A strategy worth trying, to reduce your interest rate or to avoid paying a higher rate on your credit card balances is:

Call the 800 number on the back of your card and politely ask the bank to make you a more attractive offer, pointing out that you've been a good customer-if you have. In all likelihood, you'll get your wish without much fuss.

If the bank refuses to lower your rate, call back in a few weeks once you have looked into offers made by the card issuer's competition. GetSmart.com offers a helpful credit card finder, free, as well as BankRate.com.

If the bank card operator still denies you a lower rate-even after you mention the competition-politely but firmly point out that you plan to cancel the card.

Seven Habits of Highly Effective Savers

Other people are so busy trying to impress you that they will, at best, not notice your efforts to impress them. At worst, they will resent you for one-upping them.

- *Highly effective savers don't try to impress other people.* They are clear about their priorities and spend money on what is important to them, like their church, education and travel.
- *They don't go shopping as a hobby, but instead go for a specific item that they need.*
- *Highly effective savers live within their means, buying only what they can afford.* (Note: There is room for more luxury when you have socked away enough for security. We don't have to be total Puritans after all!)
- *Highly effective savers take care of what they have, including their own bodies.*
- *They wear out things before replacing them.* However, they do replace them before the item requires so much care that it's wearing *them* out. If your car, for example, is costing more hours and money in repairs than it's giving you in service, do buy a newer one.
- *Often, they are do-it-yourselfers.* Just ask yourself before you hire an expert, "Can I do it myself?"
- *Highly effective savers research their purchases and comparison-shop.* They take advantage of coupons and special sales.

You probably know seventy times seven habits of highly effective savers. Pick some to incorporate into your life. When your financial foundation is sturdy cut loose a little and buy some goodies that truly mean something to you.

Summary: Chapter 8
Dealing With Debt

- *Draw on discipline and creativity to reduce your expenses.*
- *Develop a debt reduction plan.*
- *Learn to handle credit wisely.*
- *Get professional help when it's needed.*

Nine

The Dirty Dozen of Finance

Do you feel like you're guilty of malpractice when it comes to managing your money? It's no wonder.

We do not get training in handling finances, parenting, or staying married, three of the most important jobs we'll ever have. We get drivers' training, but no Basic Parenting. We're taught how to write resumes and we receive job training, but not how to manage our money or our marriages.

If you chose your parents well, you are taught by example. Sometimes it's by horrible example, but learning is learning. You watch what they do and decide not to do the same because you don't like the results.

Two of the jobs, marriage and parenting, you more or less volunteer to do. You can avoid them. But you do not sign up for money management. It is thrust upon you, ready or not. Unless you opt to sign away all your worldly goods and take up living in a Fifteenth Century style religious community, you have personal financial matters to handle on a daily basis.

It is a bad deal to see high-quality human beings in distress because of finances. For those who weren't handed a chart at birth for navigating the financial seas and avoiding the deadly shipwrecking rocks, I've listed a dozen big ones that crop up again and again. Ta-Da! ...Drum roll, please...

The Dirty Dozen of Finance

- The Get-Rich-Quick Syndrome
- Churning and other Commission Sins
- Fraud, Larceny, Forgery and Your Advisors
- Day Trading
- Timeshares
- Plastic Prisons
- Trading Enthusiasm for Info and Integrity
- Telephone Solicitations
- Not Asking; Not Knowing
- Vehicle Trap
- Trying to Fill a Void with Money
- Bad Habits Anonymous

*Note The last two of the "financial Dirty Dozen" are highly subjective. Feel free to just "Stick to the facts, Ma'am!" Skip them if that's not your thing. If it is, you'll probably feel more at ease with this whole concept for reading them.

The Get-Rick-Quick Syndrome "It's going to the moon!" a friend touting his latest hot stock enthuses. Surely, there's a short cut to wealth!

One of our Great American Dreams dies hard. It's the twin brother of "overnight success." *Get rich quick.* Neither one holds up under close scrutiny. Talk about Lady Luck being fickle! These boys will break your heart.

We know, intellectually, that we should not give money to someone without checking on them, but the glitter of easy riches can blind us. They're more alluring than the work ethic, more glamorous than saving.

Is winning the lottery part of your financial plan? I used to collect hard luck stories of lottery winners. I don't mean how tough they had it before winning, but after.

Go ahead and "play" the lottery, the slots, the horses, the pork belly futures, the derivatives, and try the short selling of the stock market, if you must. List it under "Entertainment." If by chance you win, be prepared to deal with your new responsibilities and challenges.

If you really believe you can beat the odds, get ready for your jackpot by learning how to handle money. In the meantime, invest most of your money in something less risky. You can invest in some mutual funds for as little as $50 a month with an initial investment of $250.and the odds on your investment paying off are in your favor.

Here's one example:

Lottery Winner Not So Lucky

PITTSBURGH (AP) - A man whose lottery jackpot brought him nothing but hard luck, persuaded a judge Thursday to auction off the $4.9 million he would have collected over the next 17 years.

"I want to get rid of the lottery, believe me, Your Honor. It's really been a pain," William "Bud" Post, who won the Pennsylvania Lottery in 1988, told Bankruptcy Judge Judith K. Fitzgerald before Thursday's auction.

Post said he needs the money right away to pay medical bills for an undisclosed health problem and to appeal an assault conviction (and a two- to six-year prison term) for firing a gun to scare his step-daughter's boyfriend. Since he hit it big, Post's brother has been convicted of trying to kill him, his sixth wife moved out on him, and his landlady won a lawsuit for one-third of Post's winnings.

Market Timing People try to buy at a low point and sell when a stock's price is high. Brokers can get rich that way, because of the commissions at every point of sale. (See "Churning.")

Tom Henry, a broker with Smith Barney in San Francisco told radio listeners, that "People are their own worst enemy. ...they see a short-term market fluctuation (stock prices dropping temporarily) and they think that proves...that the world can come to an end...That's the time to keep your investments in place like you were wearing lead shoes."

All the books, magazines, and newsletters that tell you when to buy or sell will almost always underperform a "standpatter" who stays fully invested in good quality stock funds and continues to save and invest.

Warren Buffett, the most successful investor in the world, says his favorite length of time to keep a stock is "forever."

"Ponzi" schemes Investors are led to believe they will get rich without risk. If something sounds too good to be true, it probably is.

Ponzi was a Boston swindler who came as an immigrant to New York City at age 20, penniless and established a worthless company with the imposing name of "Securities Exchange Company."

He offered "investments" redeemable in 90 days at 50 percent interest at a time when Boston banks were paying 4 percent annual interest. The newspapers were quick to point that the postal coupons he offered to buy overseas and sell in America at a huge profit were not capable of doing that. There weren't enough postal coupons in the world to make that kind of money! Eager investors nevertheless poured as much as $15 million into the Securities Exchange Company.

The scheme could continue to work, Ponzi knew, only as long as the interest earned by previous investors was paid out of the money received from subsequent investors, with him pocketing the difference. When that was not possible the so-called investors lost everything.

Remember the comic strip "Calvin and Hobbes"? It was an education in itself. Calvin is sweating over his homework, as Hobbes the wise tiger, strolls up:

> Calvin: "Everything is so darn hard. I wish I could just take a pill to be perfect and I wish I could just push a button to have anything I want. Why should I have to work for everything? It's like saying I don't deserve it."
> Hobbes: "The American Dream lives on."

So it does. I believe in miracles. I just think most of the time you have to work to make them happen. Do you think you can sit on a rock and think prosperous thoughts to create wealth and security? Please reconsider. It's a good beginning, but you can't quit there.

Solution: Recognize that "get rich quick schemes" are a pretty shaky underpinning for your finances.

Investigate thoroughly any investment, but double your questions if it sounds "too good to be true." You know the rest of the cliché'. Cliché's don't usually last unless there's at least a germ of truth to them. Don't let greed blind you. Get a second opinion.

Churning Churning is defined as excessive buying and selling of stocks by a broker.

"Churning sound might be broker getting richer" read the headline of Linda Sterms' financial column. "Despite the recent growth of fee-based financial advice and the popularity of buy-and-hold investing, there are still some unsavory brokers bilking their clients out of thousands of dollars in commissions."

She detailed three horror stories of clients who turned over their money to a broker they didn't know very well. What did these victims have in common besides the loss of their money? Greed, sure. Laziness, too, and the belief that somebody they don't even know can be trusted to make them rich in a hurry.

Even active mutual fund managers rarely turn over or sell and replace an entire portfolio more than once a year. State-of-the-art investment theory maintains that the less you trade the better. Every sale takes money out of your pocket.

Attorney Dennis Villvicencio of Carlsbad, California, who makes a living representing clients who have been wronged by brokers states that if your portfolio changes more than twice a year there's an inference that your broker was churning. If it turns over more than four times a year, the broker has to prove he wasn't churning.

And, if your holdings change six times in one year, existing cases have held that this was "conclusive" evidence of churning.

Solution: Check out your financial advisor carefully (See Dirty Dozen #3).

Check every trade and every statement and add up the commissions that your account is creating. If your broker starts making more than you do, look out!

Fraud, Larceny, Forgery Most people expect their brokers to be a combination of wizard, saint and psychic. They're likely to be disappointed.

The most a full-service broker can do is offer advice about strategies and recommend promising securities.

Unfortunately, brokers are torn by conflicting desires. They want to add to your wealth, but they also want your stock trading to increase their commissions. You, therefore, have to approach a broker with a mixture of faith and distrust.

You can avoid any conflict of interest by using a discount brokerage firm such as Charles Schwab, or Quick & Reilly, but you have to do some research and thinking on your own. You also need to buy five hundred shares or more to save money with discounters because they charge a minimum fee per order.

You can pay very low maintenance fees, 0.18 percent, about one-fifth of a percent, for example, and buy shares of an index fund. Once you buy it, you stay in it. Statistics show a superior return for this scenario in most cases. (See Chapter 12, "Fine Tuning.") Taxes are lower when you don't buy and sell repeatedly.

If you're about to join the "in-crowd" with someone who can triple the return you can get anywhere else, or who has a hot stock or a pile of dirt (guaranteed to contain gold, of course), *stop*! Don't make a move toward your checkbook until you:

- Check out the offer with a financial planner or accountant before you trust your money to someone you don't know.
- Be aware that by using false authorization letters, scam artists can transfer your investments to bank under their own name. Glowing returns can be based on falsified brokerage or other in-house statements.
- Remember that though the Securities and Exchange Commission (SEC) might catch the wrong-

doers, it is not empowered to recover and return any fraud losses to investors.

Work with a full-service broker. Select at least three firms that: have been in business at least ten years; are members of the New York Stock Exchange; and belong to the Securities Investor Protection Corporation.

Meet the branch manager, explain your investment goals and ask the manager to recommend a specific individual.

Interview the broker, asking questions like:

- When did you become a broker? The more bear (down) and bull (up) market swings he's weathered, the more expert he'll be at responding.
- What's your investment approach? Does it make sense, and does it agree with yours?
- What investment products do you specialize in? Be leery of investments that are wildly speculative, such as penny stocks, commodities, and options, or those that carry high commissions or fees such as closed-end mutual funds, gold and real estate limited partnerships.
- What stocks have you bought recently and why? Do you own those stocks? See if you are comfortable with his explanation.
- What are your firm's commission rates? The normal amount is 1 percent of the principal. Do you discount commissions for good customers?
- What other fees does your firm charge? Processing and handling fees, charges for sending out stock certificates, levies on inactive accounts are some possible fees.
- Does your firm offer an asset management account? What other products and services does

your firm offer? Some firms, like Merrill Lynch, are like a financial mall.

After the interview, verify the broker's credentials. Call the North American Securities Administrators hot line at 800-942-9022 for the number to see if the broker is registered with the National Association of Securities Dealers. Ask to be read the broker's CRD file-the Central Registration Depository report. This file tells how long a broker has been in business, where he has worked and for how long, and whether disciplinary actions have ever been brought against him. (You can even obtain a record of any federal complaints from SEC's Freedom of Information Branch, 450 Fifth St. NW, Mail Stop 2-6, Washington, D.C. 20549. If you want to go that far.)

When you've decided on a broker, give him a written list of goals and update them periodically, including the rate of return you expect. Stress that you want a quarterly performance review and that you want to be alerted when to buy as well as when to sell.

Initially, turn down a margin account, which lets you borrow from your broker to buy stock, or a discretionary account, which gives the broker authority to invest without your knowledge or consent. Invest a small sum until your broker proves himself. Confirm in a letter any conversations by phone.

Finally, check monthly statements for accuracy, performance and charges.

Contact the broker right away if you spot questionable items, or you may lose your legal right to damages. If your broker is not topping the prevailing rate of one-year T-bills, look for another broker.

Day Trading The recent tragedy in Atlanta in which a man, distraught from financial losses, killed nine people at two brokerage houses is an extreme response to the pressures brought on by the new phenomenon of day trading. (That's buying and selling a position within a day.) The Internet makes it easy and the ads are seductive.

Not everyone who trades stocks on line is a day trader.

Accessing brokerages on line makes sense for most people, especially when commissions can be low for investing transactions. Day trading may look like investing, but it's far from it.

How do day traders perform? A recent study by the North American Securities Administrators Association suggests that only about 11.5 percent might trade profitably, and they are stuck paying the higher short-term capital gains rate.

Mitchell Freedman is a veteran financial planner, immediate past chairman of the California Society of CPAs Personal Planning Committee, and founder of an accountancy corporation in Sherman Oaks, California. Here's his view of day trading: "Of course there are stories of people who have made money trading securities.... However, I'm the guy that clients can't fool, because when I prepare their income tax returns I see the results of their trading activities...It never ceases to amaze me how clients conveniently forget to mention their losses during these conversations."

He continues, "...the majority of individuals realize that they can't become rich or even make reasonable amounts of money trading securities. Even with low transaction costs from discount brokers, the sheer volume of trades generated by short term activity is costly...Furthermore, if you're lucky enough to gain, the taxes will kill you. ...the trader must consistently achieve substantially better results than the long-term investor to accomplish the same net (after tax and transaction costs) results. And let me tell you, that rarely happens."

The people who appear to be making the biggest killing in day trading are those running day trading firms. Regulators are investigating this industry.

What can I say after that? Not much, except if you need to get the trading bug out of your system, pick out a small, expendable portion of your personal fortune and "play" with it. Examine the consequences over long periods of time. And keep most of your money working for you, elsewhere.

Timeshares Maybe you love your time share, and that's fine. This, however, is a list of Dirty Dozen of Finance. As an investment, time shares flunk, no matter what the salesman said.

In fairness, I also must say that I have friends who have enjoyed their time shares immensely, and so have we as their guests. Also, some people might not make time for vacations without time share schedules motivating them.

Is there any reason to consider a time share as a real estate investment? Absolutely not. The problem is, time is not property. The right to use something for a specified period of time is not equivalent to owning property, even if it does offer some of the tax write-offs that second homes do.

The sales practices of time share sales people are infamous.

Ask John Linkous of Chesterton, Indiana. He is already into the second year of dealing with the nightmare that time shares sales can become, a nightmare that finds him stuck with a deal he cannot afford to keep and finds impossible to resell.

The time share people made a lot of promises to John, none of which he says came true.

A valuable product does not require high-pressure sales techniques.

- Solution: For the best bargains on time shares, if they fit into your life style, buy from owners not from property developers.
- Time shares lose value quickly, so plenty of owners are trying to sell them for pennies on the dollar. That is where the best opportunities lie.
- Search classified ads from Timeshare Users Group, (904) 264-3512 or www.tug2.net, and TimeSharing Today Magazine, (201) 871-4304 or www.tstoday.com.
- Never put money down until you make sure the description is accurate.
- Visit the property yourself.

If everything checks out, make a low counteroffer to the listed price.

Source: David and Linda Glickstein, editors, *The Discerning Traveler*

Plastic Prison When I was in college, tobacco companies used to pass out free samples of cigarettes. I'm happy to see that more restrictions are placed on their activities now.

A similar lure, credit cards, are being dangled in front of unsophisticated users.

Most of us have experienced how easy it is to get imprisoned by your plastic in a prison of debt.

Money rules change and even sophisticated credit card users may be surprised at some developments since 1997.

"Credit Card users get stung by killer fees." columnist Ann Perry writes. According to her, credit card companies are trying hard to boost their lackluster profits by:

- Piling on new fees

- Jacking up old ones
- And adopting a hair-trigger response to enforcing all that fine print in the card contract.

One slip, such as being a day late on your payment, and you could be hit with a $29 penalty. And that 3.9 percent introductory interest rate of yours could rocket to 18 percent or more overnight.

What happened? While millions of Americans remain mired in consumer debt, a surprising number no longer carry a balance from month to month. In the early 1990's, when the economy was poor, 71 percent of credit card holders carried a balance. Now the percentage is 58 and falling. That's a growing problem for the industry.

Watch for:

- Higher Late Payment fees, with due date strictly enforced
- Shorter Grace Periods
- Fees for exceeding credit limits
- Penalty interest rates
- Penalties for your behavior with other creditors
- New or increased rates on cash advances
- Increased currency fees (on overseas purchases)
- Inactivity fees (For example, customers who don't use their card enough could be subjected to a $1 a month fee, failure to pay off the $1 can result in a late fee, which in turn can trigger the higher interest rate penalty. All for doing nothing.)

Solutions:

- Reduce the number of cards to one or two, lessening the chance of misplacing a statement and triggering a fee.

- Use credit cards only when absolutely necessary or when other means are inconvenient.
- When getting a new card, choose one with a longer grace period.
- Open statements as soon as they arrive. Pay immediately.
- Reduce your balances to avoid exceeding limits.
- If you plan to travel abroad, check with your company to learn the surcharge policy.
- Mail payments promptly.
- If you've held the card for some time, check on current policies.
- Check your credit rating once a year. Write or call TRW (now Experian) or other credit bureau for the once a year free copy.

Credit Bureaus (for free reports)

EQUIFAX
P.O. Box 740241
Atlanta, GA 30374-0241
(800) 685-1111
Order online at equifax.com

EXPERIAN (Formerly TRW)
P.O. Box 949
Allen, TX 75013-0949
(888) 397-3742
experian.com

Trans Union Corporation
Consumer Disclosure Center
P.O. Box 390
Springfield, PA 19064-0390
(800) 916-8800
tuc.com

Trading Enthusiasm for Info and Integrity Many salesmen, brokers and other representatives of the financial world exude confidence and excitement. You catch fire from their attitudes and glowing descriptions.

They are far more interesting than the ones who pepper their presentations with disclaimers and "wet the blanket" with their cautionary tales.

It is important to look beyond the puff and flash at the facts underlying. The older you are the more susceptible you may be. That nice salesman who came all the way across town to see you still needs to be accountable.

A simple solution: Get a second opinion from someone you trust.

Telephone Solicitations Why would you want to trust your money to a complete stranger who calls up to solicit your business?

Maybe I'm naïve, but wouldn't the better deals (for the consumer, that is) have people lining up to take advantage of them? As in *Build a better mouse trap, and the world will beat a path to your door*? Or did I get that right?

If the offer sounds irresistible, you can always check it out by asking for mailings, credentials, and personal meetings. However, we have an ironclad rule, sort of like the "Don't talk to strangers" for children. It is "Sorry, we never accept any solicitations of any kind over the phone. Not interested. Have a nice day. (That last sentence is optional.) Click."

Not Asking; Not Knowing Some people brag that they never open the statements from their brokerage accounts. It's as though they can't sully their minds with the sordid details of how much money their broker is raking in for them. I guess they're above all that.

Ten Safe Investments You Can Make In Twenty Minutes Or Less

For Ten Safe Investments that don't require your constant supervision, check this list that Mary L. Sprouse recommended in *If Time Is Money, No Wonder I'm Not Rich*. These investments are discussed in Chapter 12, "Fine Tuning."

- EE Savings Bonds
- Certificates of Deposit
- Money Market Mutual Funds
- Bank Money Market Accounts
- U.S. Treasury Issues
- Ginnie Mae Certificates
- Ginnie Mae Mutual Funds
- Ginnie Mae Unit Investment Trusts
- Stock Mutual Funds
- Blue-Chip Stocks

Another version of this is "I don't have a clue about our finances. (*Fill in name*) handles all that." What if (*fill in name*) dies? Or runs off? If (*fill in name*) cares about you, I hope he/she/it tries harder to involve and educate you.

Don't ever tell your broker that you want him to handle everything, that you are too busy to be bothered, even if it's true.

If you're that busy, I recommend passive investments that you can leave alone, that won't crash and burn the moment you take your eyes off them.

The saddest aspect of this sort of financial blunder is when someone wants to know, and is afraid to ask questions. You NEED to ask questions. There are no dumb questions. That's how you learn. Repeat after me, "I will ask questions when I don't understand something." (Can you tell I'm a "recovering teacher"?)

Seriously, there's something very wrong somewhere when anyone who is dealing with your money is resistant to questions. It's a form of disrespect. You have a right to know.

Don t let them "dis" you, as the kids used to say in the inner city schools.

Once I was invited to visit an investment club. During a two-hour session, I asked two questions, one of which was answered.

The woman organizing the club suggested afterward that maybe the club wasn't a good fit for me because they had to be decisive, to move along quickly and that she didn't have time to answer a lot of questions. She was absolutely right about one thing. The club was definitely not a good fit!

I'd like to hear some good investment club stories from readers (as well as any other kind). To be honest, I don't have any. That doesn't mean the good stories aren't out there, so enlighten me.

If people involved in handling your money are in your family and, up until now, you've never wanted or needed to be involved, you will have some major adjustments to make.

I think it's important that the money manager understand that trust is not the issue, assuming it isn't, and that criticism is not the intent. We all have a streak of wanting to defend our domains, control our castles, barricade our bar racks...Oops, I got carried away.

I'll leave it up to you to convey the message that you're just trying to grow up a little, assume some responsibility, or whatever's true for you.

What if trust is an issue? I'd say seek outside help. Sometimes there's good reason for one person in the family to be excluded from financial responsibilities,

Does that fit you? If so, you will have to earn back that trust by a series of consistent and responsible financial actions.

Assuming you're not the untrustworthy one, talk to someone neutral that you respect and describe your situation.

Often, far more than finances are involved, so I don't know which kind of intervention or support to suggest. It would vary, depending on the problems. Most people know what the problem is, or suspect it.

Once you have figured that out, and admitted that you are dealing with a particular issue, then action steps to solve the problem can be identified. (See "Name it, Claim it, Tame it" in Chapter 3.) It's amazing how much support and help is waiting for you when you truly focus on solving a problem. Solutions start coming out of the very walls!

Vehicle Trap I'm really asking for it. Not only do I live in Car Country U.S.A. commonly known as Southern California, but I love my little Mustang. I'm going to say it anyway.

Cars, trucks, boats, planes, campers and recreational vehicles are not assets.

They may have other redeeming qualities, but they are not a good investment. Many of us know this on an intellectual level. When it comes to a portfolio, those little old ladies driving their 13 year old Camrys may be laughing all the way to the bank, discreetly of course.

Through experience, I learned that the couples with the Mercedes and SUVs adorning their driveways often had hidden accessories to go with their acquisitions. Debt and financial drain were not optional but standard equipment on their vehicles.

And boats! They're almost a separate category of financial disaster themselves...and lest you think I'm just an old killjoy who doesn't know what I'm talking about, we (*blush*) have one. It is indefensible, which is just what Warren Buffett dubbed his corporate jet, "The Indefensible." As one of the richest men in the world, he can afford it. Most of us can't.

Not only is a vehicle costly to buy or lease, there are also often the costs of cleaning, maintenance and repair, insurance, registration, taxes, depreciation, licenses, parking (and sometimes tickets/fines), interest on loans, accidents, gas and oil, and parts and accessories.

We have two dear and unconventional friends who pride themselves in making their vehicles last. One of them, a doctor, put new engines in his beloved orange Volkswagen until he finally, after twenty years or so, had to buy another car. Maybe he has some kind of world's record.

We're simply outclassed by people like that. Keep the vehicle habit in check. It can do you in.

If you're really determined to save money. Park the gas-guzzler permanently and use alternate forms of transportation.

Do we know you're not going to do that? At least, don't buy a new car. Get one "new" to you and pocket the difference. Better yet, *invest* the difference.

Trying to Fill a Void with Money Here's the bottom line:

If you don't feel good about yourself, you will be trying to compensate with money, one way or another.

Sometimes it's by buying affection or demanding monetary tokens of affection. Do you feel you can't take someone out unless you can spring for the most expensive restaurant dinner? Do you not date unless someone will take you first class?

Sometimes it's by having to show off the latest, biggest, most expensive, or largest collection of (fill in the blank). (Note: I have the world s largest collection of sea shells. I keep it scattered on beaches all over the world. Maybe you ve seen some of it?)

Sometimes it's by doing a financial version of anorexia nervosa where no matter how rich you get, you always feel poor. You are driven the way the characters were in the haunting short story, "The Rocking Horse Winner" by D.H. Lawrence, by a voice that wails, "There must be more money!" You are the misers and "Scrooges." There's never enough.

Sometimes it's by spending to make yourself feel better. You don't really long for another pair of shoes. You long for something in yourself that you don't have or haven't been able to find. You're a "Splurger."

Sometimes it's feeling needy because of deprivation in the past. You want to make it up to yourself, or spoil your kids. "

The Lady Bountiful syndrome is using gifts to those less privileged to make one feel superior. Sometimes food is even taken out of the family pantry or dollars from the rent money to "help others."

I'm not against helping others, and have done my share. From a financial standpoint, an injudicious gift of money can enable and weaken both giver and receiver. The litmus test for Lords and Ladies Bountiful is "Am I able to receive graciously?" and "Am I doing something for someone that they are capable of doing themselves?" It's lonely up there on the throne.

Solution to the Problem of the Void: Seek professional help if necessary, but deal with the root problem or problems so you can get on with a good life. You'll need a support group, official or unofficial.

Find the missing or buried piece of you. *Every* aspect of your life will prosper.

Bad Habits Anonymous When I was training for a counseling certificate, something we were taught really stuck in my mind. I observed the truth of it repeatedly.

What we were advised was that if someone in a relationship was abusing drugs or suffering some kind of addiction, that it was necessary to deal with that and clear It up before appreciable progress could be made in their relationships.

Your relationship with money is no exception. Horror stories of drug addicts and what they will do to obtain money to support their habit are common.

I believe any harmful addiction is the same way. Imagine trying to balance a budget if you're addicted to gambling, cocaine, sex, shopping, overeating, or any habit that controls you more than you control it. Okay, so we all have lapses...but I'm talking a matter of degree, here. If it interferes with your life, it's harmful. Chances are an occasional candy bar does not.

I started smoking in college and went through agonies of withdrawal in order to quit eight years later. There's no way I could concentrate on my financial well being during that period.

While I was smoking, there was no way I could do without the cigarettes...no matter what the cost.

Here's a personal gambling story:

A sweet, grandmotherly friend contacted me when I worked for Principal Financial Group. Seems that the "boys" (actually in their 30's and 40's) who managed her motel for her had finally hit it big in Las Vegas. She wanted me to help them invest it, since they had never had a pile of money before and she was mothering them.

I met the "boys," and was entertained by their miraculous story of putting in three quarters and winning $20,000.

I had to talk very persuasively to get them to put even 25 percent into an investment. They had debts. They weren't sure just how much they had lost in Las Vegas before the magic moment.

A few months passed. At 7:30 one morning I received a hurried call that they were leaving town for good. Somebody's mother was seriously ill and they needed their money in a hurry. The arrangements were made. They were gone in a cloud of dust.

Later that week my friend called. Did I know where "the boys" had gone? They had helped themselves to the motel money to cover gambling debts and then skipped town. They took more than her money. I think they broke a piece off her heart.

Keep a lid on recreational gambling. Be honest about how much you've lost.

If you find yourself lying about your losses and winnings, stop gambling. If you can't stop, get help. Gamblers Anonymous offers a list of questions to evaluate your gambling. You can contact them at isomain@gamblersanonymouslorg or visit their home page at gamblersanonymous.org on the Web, also.

Most of us can help ourselves to a great extent, but often need support and help to break a bad habit. It is even more urgent to seek professional and personal help in overcoming an addiction.

Getting your timing down can have an effect on your finances. Either waiting too long or jumping too soon makes a difference. Sometimes these are habitual approaches to life and decision making.

Have you missed out on some important things in your life because you waited too long? You may have a habit of procrastination.

Are you often regretting a move you made without thinking it through or doing due diligence? Perhaps it's laziness or impulsiveness. Chances are, you know whether it's out of control or excessive for you.

"Do it now!" makes a good motto, but does not void the necessity of checking on investment decisions and getting all the facts verified.

The real scoop is that any habit or addiction that interferes with a balanced life is detrimental to your financial well being.

Summary, Chapter 9
The Dirty Dozen Of Finance

- *Plan your finances and check out all investments carefully.*
- *Don't talk to strangers about your money.*
- *Rid yourself of harmful addictions.*
- *Educate yourself about your finances; ask questions.*
- *Don't let car costs "drive" you to ruin.*
- *Work on getting emotional needs satisfied.*
- *Don't depend on money for love, attention, respect or understanding.*

Ten

Home on the Range

Do you remember the words of the old song, *Home on the Range*? "...where never is heard a discouraging word, and the skies are not cloudy all day."

It is high time to recognize your achievements and to give you permission to avoid perfection.

Just as one day of eating junk food doesn't mean you're doomed to a life of poor health and excess weight, you are allowed days where you don't toe the financial line.

It doesn't matter, in the larger scheme of things.

What does matter is your general direction.

Let's tally up some of your accomplishments already:

- You began to form the thoughts that result in action.
- You read this book this far.
- You started being more aware of money.
    You recognized some emotions around finances.
- You may have actually taken some action steps,

Congratulations! That's how it begins.

I want to tell you two stories, one personal and short, the other classic.

The personal one is simply that I've managed to incorporate a daily walk-a good thing-into my life.

I've done this, although I am more spontaneous than disciplined, with the following motto: "Something is better than nothing."

I bow respectfully to those who simply form a habit and "Just do it."

On days when the last thing in the world I want to do is exercise, I cajole myself outside with my motto.

I might even say to myself, "Just to the corner." Often, once I begin, it is not so bad. It might even turn out to be fun. I don't feel guilty if I don't go the last mile. After all, something is better than nothing.

Thus, I've remained healthy. I'm not holding up this as a perfect routine, but it works for me. It works in money matters, too. Maybe I don't save and invest $500 a month more, but am I investing more? Planning more? Saving more?

The other story is from *An Autobiography in Five Short Chapters*, by Portia Nelson:

Chapter One: I walk down the street and come to a deep hole in the sidewalk. I fall in; I feel lost-helpless, but it's not my fault. It takes forever to find my way out.

Chapter Two: I walk down the same street and come to a deep hole in the sidewalk. I pretend I don't see it, and fall in again. I can't believe I'm in the same place-but it isn't my responsibility. It still takes a long time to get out.

Chapter Three: I walk down the same street and come to a deep hole in the sidewalk. I see it-but I still fall in. By now it's a habit. But my eyes are open; I know where I am. I take full responsibility. I get out immediately.

Chapter Four: I walk down the same street and come to a deep hole in the sidewalk. I walk around it.

Chapter Five: I walk down another street.

I don't know where you are in your chapters; I do know that you can "walk down another street." Maybe you won't get that far in a week, month or even a year, but you would not still be reading these words without some motivation.

Congratulations! Take time out to assess what you have decided or sensed about your own situation.

Now, maybe you are full of energy and direction. If that is the case, plunge right into the "Kindergarten Filing System" chapter so you can launch your new financial freedom and build your wealth and security.

However, maybe you are overwhelmed. This is for you.

Let's start with possible positions you might identify with at this point. Pick one:

- "My life's a mess. I don't know where to begin."
- "I'm my own worst enemy when it comes to money; I know better but I keep on making the same mistakes."
- "I start out all enthused, and then sort of grind to a halt. Then I'm back right where I started, broke and out-of-control."
- Other.

Well, what's the answer to your dilemma? You thought I was going to tell you, didn't you? I'm a firm believer in the concept that an individual knows herself better than I do and knows what to do in a situation, if she gives it some thought.

I'm only able to tell you what has worked for others and me in my experience. I offer it to you in all humility.

The last word belongs to one of my clients, who is turning her finances in a better direction. I called her about a month after we met.

I asked her if she was happier about her money situation. "Yes!" she said firmly. "What made the difference?" was my next question. "Making the decision." was her instant reply.

She told me that she had made a decision that she was tired of her money struggles. She was willing to take some action. Some shift within her took place.

Just as clearly as a weather vane responds to a change of wind direction, her life began to change.

All sorts of help and opportunities entered her life as a result.

It can happen for you, if it hasn't already.

It starts with your decision.

Summary—Chapter 10

Home on the Range

- *Give yourself credit.*
- *Celebrate any progress.*
- *Decide for once and for all, that you will take action on your finances.*

Eleven

The Kindergarten Filing System

Are you having fun yet? Probably not if every money move you try to make is hampered by "Where is it?" "What is it?" and "When did (or should) that happen?"

Have I got a deal for you! Unlike all the organized folks who really love shuffling through papers, most of us don't love it.

Well, there are very simple, if unorthodox, ways to "get organized." I'll even let you pick the level that is most comfortable for you.

Level A is the simplest. It also doesn't work quite as well as Level Z, but it is easier, takes less time, costs less and it will get you through.

Most problems with money and organization crop up in these areas:

- Finding the piece of paper you need
- Crunching the numbers; Adding the money.
- Meeting deadlines.

- Retrieving information

If you are already good at the above, please spare me some embarrassment and skip this section. I am not an expert. However, I have worked out a system that works beautifully for me, with the help of many kind friends, and it transformed me.

My premise is that if it worked for me, and I was hopeless, then it might help someone else who needs a Kindergarten level of mastery. Remember the book *All I Really Need to Know I Learned in Kindergarten* by Robert Fulghum? Well, this is all you need to know about filing, and it is basic. I still squirm when someone says to me, "You're so organized!" I will probably never reach anyone's ideal, but I'm functioning.

Level A: Holding Life Together With Giant Paper Clips

Find a shoe box, or if you've been really active this year financially, a boot box. Write the current year on all sides with a bold, permanent felt point pen.

Put all financial records in the box. If you don't like shifting through all the papers every time, put them in labeled envelopes according to what they are or clamp them in groups with a giant paper clip.

Change boxes at the end of the year.

Start fresh with the New Year.

Store last year's boxes in a dry, accessible place in chronological order. Repeat process each year. Keep only seven years worth of records on hand. Shred the old records.

Exceptions to Keep Forever

- Deed to your home
- Receipts for IRA contributions

- Diplomas
- Certificates of Birth, Marriage; Passports)
- Social Security Card
- Pictures of your grandparents
- Current Insurance Policies
- Registration/ "pink slips" for vehicles
- Stock and bond certificates
- Titles to current property
- Documents relating to all home sales.

Put them in your cheap, fire-resistant safe or safe deposit box.

The advantage to the one-box system is that you have only one place to look for anything current.

The disadvantage is that you have to paw through it all, every time you need a certain piece of paper.

Obviously, what we need is a big box of jumbo paper clips. You can sort the papers into categories and clip them together…which sounds suspiciously like filing. That brings us to…

My Favorite System: Level Z

The system has the following components:

- Reducing the amount of paper.
- Filing necessary paper or information in a user-friendly system.
- Keeping the system up to date.

Reducing the Amount of Paper I use the one-touch TAF (T for Toss; A for Act; F for File) system. If I touch it, I must toss it, file it or take action on it…immediately, unless I can delegate (refer) it. Then it becomes TRAF, Toss, Refer, Act or File.

Ideally, it would take place the moment I receive it. For "those days" when I am severely pressed for time, I have four baskets:

- waste paper basket (The Round File)
- action (Things to do right away.)
- file (Things to store.)
- refer, "for someone else's hands" (Things to delegate.)

I always sort mail standing next to a wastebasket. If I am concerned about preserving my privacy from the dumpster divers, I rip the papers in two and put one half in one basket and the other outside in the trash collection bin. A more sophisticated approach would be to use a paper shredder, I suppose.

When I touch a paper in a file, I toss it in the Round File if it is outdated. We also clean out our files every year, whether they need it or not!

But, stay tuned. My version of "cleaning them out" is not labor.

Starting the System First, pick a color: blue or "yuck green." Those are the only two colors I've been able to find for hanging files. (I must admit I haven't made a big effort to find other hues.)

Next, purchase a two-drawer filing cabinet from Office Depot or Staples, or use some thrifty alternative for a filing cabinet.

While you're there, you'll need some hanging files (in your color choice) and some file folders. Perhaps you can rustle up these items another way. The hanging files require a frame. (Call me. I ended up with too many of them...or buy your own.)

I've tried filing without hanging files and my folders always end up bent and collapsed in a sad heap.

Putting papers in the folders was a pain, until I tried the hanging versions that just slide easily and open wide to receive the new offering.

Next, find two pieces of paper and put the alphabet on one, writing with a pencil, leaving spaces between every 3 or 4 letters for you to write. This will be the list of your Business files' contents. Mine looks like this:

Business File Contents
ABC
   24-Hour Fitness
   AAA
   Auto
   Boat
DEF
   DMV
   Donations
   Fees, etc.

The categories are as broad as possible. The file names begin with a noun. Otherwise, I'll lose them. I found that out when "Prospects, New" was useful as a title, but "New Prospects" was apt to get lost in my packed file cabinet.

For example, I have an "Insurance" file that contains life, auto, home, landlord's, liability, life and health insurance. If it is insurance, it's in there.

I use the jumbo paper clips to keep the categories separate.

"Medical" contains Dentist and Doctor records, exam results, health tips from the Internet.

Whenever I put a piece of paper in the file, I put it in the rear of the folder consistently so that the data is sequential.

Other broad categories are Home Improvement, Donations, Newspapers/Magazines; Taxes, Utilities, Telephones, MBNA (our one credit card), Gifts, and Donations.

Since the list of contents is in pencil, you can add or erase or change as you place the contents list in the very front of the file. (I staple mine to a folder, which you can get in some gorgeous colors.) The reason for the list is that I don't always remember my categories when facing a new piece of paper to file. It also helps your partner find and file material.

In a separate drawer, keep your bank and bills related files:

Bills To Pay
Checking
Deposits To Be Made, Gift Certificates
Income Tax Returns (Dated)
Savings (Even I don't need a contents list for this file.)

Once a bill is paid, the receipt goes into the Business File

I established a file for checks to be deposited the day after we spent hours combing through the trash searching for an errant check. You minimalists can put those checks directly into your wallet.

The bill-paying drawer and the Business file are the day-to-day finances. The second file is for your investments and permanent records. Here's the way I have it set up:

Guarantees/ Owners' Manuals
Income
Investments/Retirement/Assets
   Charles Schwab
   Condo
   Dennison House
   Fidelity
   Etc.

Keep the categories broad, e.g., You may have more than one fund with Fidelity, but file all the funds with that company in the same folders. Remember the famous paper clip trick to separate the different accounts if you like.

Keeping It Up At the end of the year, buy a book box, label it with the year, put all the files in it, retrieving any records e.g. insurance policies, that relate to the new year.

Using your old contents list, label a new batch and stick them in your newly empty file. You've made a fresh start.

Cart the box to a closet where you have the last few 5-7 years of records, put them in descending order. (You're more likely to need the most recent year's records, so why not have it on top, unless you want to work out your body that way.)

Toss any file you've had for more than 7 years, after retrieving any "keep forever" documents.

Dealing With "When" Issues Before we leave files, let me suggest that you add one more drawer or file. Perhaps it can go in with your Business file, if there's room.

Purchase some folders that are tabbed with the months of the year and with tabs that have numbers of the days of the month. This is your tickler file.

It's where you place items you won't need until a certain day, but you better be able to locate it when that day comes, like airline tickets, or directions to a party or even more business-like items.

Put it in the numbered folder corresponding to the day you'll need it, when the time for retrieval is the current month.

Put items in the "month" folder of the appropriate month if the time the information is required is not the current month.

Here's a peek at the contents of mine. In the "18" folder, which stands for the eighteenth of this month, you will find the invitation and map to a company awards banquet for this month. There are airline tickets, directions to a workshop, and other October events in the next month's folder. (Actually, I don't have any other tickler items, but I wanted to impress you.)

The Best Part of the System

I have a personal organizer. It is hermetically sealed to my side. I "don't leave home without it" as the commercial goes.

I favor the Franklin/Covey system, but there are also Day Timers, Day Runners, and many others.

It has truly changed my life. The trick is to put everything you possibly can in it. What I meant to say is to avoid floating, miscellaneous bits of scrap paper; record it in your planner. That way you know where to look. I look at mine to see (on the calendar portion) where I have to be today.

I can prioritize the most important things to accomplish with a simple ABC method. This is a great stress reliever, if you chose to regard it that way.

I never get everything I want accomplished in one day, but if I get the "A" things done, I feel fine about the day.

You can plan ahead. You know where different members of the family are supposed to be for appointments. You can put down directions, ahead of time, to prepare for an important event, like taxes or a birthday. *You can make sure your time is devoted to the areas you value most.*

There are space age versions of this planning component, but, I ask you, can you put your checkbook, address book, comb and lipstick in them?

When you talk to someone, and they give you one of *those* numbers, like the order number, cancellation number, phone number or reference number, you write it down on the day you received the information.

If you, or they, require the retrieval of that info, you know where to look, because there's only one place. People by now are accustomed to someone saying, "Just a moment, let me get my calendar, or organizer."

Of course, you DO have to look at it.

The Franklin system offers a ...believe it or not...entertaining yet informative workshop on the use of their product.

The Big Three of personal planners are:

- Day Runner Inc. 800-635-5544; dayrunner.com
- Day-Timers Inc. 800-225-5005; daytimer.com
- Franklin Covey Co. 800 269-1812; franklincovey.com

A review I read by *Fast Company* entitled "Power User's Guide to Planners," recommended the Day runner Pro Business System for the International Road Warrior, who is juggling time zones, meetings around the clock, shotgunning teams in Europe and Southeast Asia.

For the Commuter, shuttling between home and office, they said the Franklin Classic meets consistent, uncomplicated planning needs. (That's for me!)

The Pocket Day-Timer, according to the reviewer, offered a package for the High Flier who is moving fast, traveling light, leaving the details to others.

Well, all you "Road Warriors" out there, unite. Beat it to one of the stores offering planners, even if it's a generic cut-rate drugstore product.

If you're like me, you'll choose instead to order on line or by phone from a catalog. Save time, gasoline, energy and sometimes, money.

(I don't mean you need to scoop up the most expensive model plus deluxe accessories.) Once a dear friend of mine decided to get her life and money under control. She loved to shop, so naturally the part that she started with involved choosing the best-looking, deluxe Italian leather organizer with matching accessories. Hundreds of dollars later, she was organized to the hilt. She also didn't have any money left, so I guess that was under control, too. P.S. She was still a dear friend, with many other sterling qualities. I'm telling this story strictly as a disclaimer, so you won't use this chapter as a rationale for a shopping spree.

Here's a story for those who think there's not enough time or money to spend on a planner:

> *A medieval castle was under siege. The King strode out to do battle, arrayed in armor, brandishing his trusty sword.*
>
> *On his way, some servants stopped the defenders of the castle to inform him that a salesman urgently requested an audience with him.*
>
> *"I don't have time to talk to any crazy salesman!" snarled the monarch. "I have a battle to fight."*
>
> *The salesman, sadly packed his wares and slipped out the back door, heading for the next castle. "Too bad. " he thought, "He could have really used this machine gun."*

You can substitute a civil war hospital, a beleaguered doctor, and a peddler of penicillin. The point is the same: Sometimes it will save lives or win the battle to purchase the right product...and, use your wits to get it at the lowest possible price.

Cyberhelp

Sometimes, I use the categories that *Quicken* suggests for filing. *Quicken* is money management software sold by Intuit, 800-433-8810, or quicken.com. This software is as friendly as a wet dog for personal use. Earlier versions seem simpler.

Other effective money management software includes *Microsoft Money* (microsoft.com) and *Managing Your Money* (mymnet.com).

I find the utility and power of the computer to help manage money valuable. I have to admit that it is possible to thrive financially without the computer and without using the Internet, but I would suffer severe withdrawal symptoms if my cybersources were terminated.

You can pay bills, balance your checkbook, monitor your spending, figure your net worth and watch your portfolio grow, among other things. You can use the Financial Planner to calculate your retirement plan, work a budget or amortize a loan. You can even update your mutual fund' prices automatically , and much, much more.

Miscellaneous

This section relates to everything else that you lose, or confuse.

Aside from being a category to avoid in your filing, I think that simple organization skills in "Miscellaneous" areas, can save you time, money and energy...three of my favorite commodities.

How do you spend the majority of your time? How can you make your life easier there?

I love to read. Part of the joy of my life is to be able to find the right book to use or to share. I hate it when I can't locate the object of my current desire quickly. We have so many books that they are housed in several different rooms, so a search became even more challenging.

Now, they are grouped, loosely, like the ones in the library using "A Loose Dewey Decimal System," which I've listed later in this chapter. (And plans for a library with shelves to the ceiling are underway.)

I cook a lot. (Or maybe it just seems like it.) My spices are alphabetically arranged for easy retrieval and I can tell when I've doubled up on something. I just have little plastic baskets labeled A-C, etc.

Once my cleaning lady, before I bought the baskets, showed me proudly how pretty the spices looked after she had reorganized them. She matched them up according to size and with an aesthetic eye. I'm not saying it wasn't attractive.

I valued her enthusiasm AND it took me an hour to put them back in "working order." Obviously, my system isn't for everyone.

I even have my canned goods arranged that way. The system works great for me. Before I settled on my "broad categories approach," I had labels on shelves for practically everything, like "coffee," "Pepsi," "juice." Now they all go under "Beverages."

There is a danger of sending house guests into fits of uncontrollable laughter, however. I'm quieter and sneakier about my efforts, now. (You, reader, are sworn to secrecy.)

Once, my brother and sister-in-law were visiting and I heard them giggling and moving around the kitchen way into the night.

The next morning, I took the lid off the sugar bowl and stared at a note buried in the shining granules stating "SUGAR," ditto in the "COFFEE" and the "CEREAL"…and then there was "LAMP" and "LIGHT SWITCH." I found labels for months afterward.

Have you ever found out that you simply don't think like a lot of other people, and sometimes don't even realize it?

I first suspected it the morning my mother-in-law dropped by and found me vacuuming the oven and having hot dogs for breakfast. I've given up the hot dogs, but I still don't see anything wrong with the former.

My husband has a need to separate his nails, bolts, screws and other hardware into various useful (I assume.) categories.

Likewise, he has a system for fishing tackle that eludes me. It is very handy, however, to be able to find whatever it is. Ask him about his system.

My point is simply that whatever you spend a lot of time doing begs for organization, so you can find it when you want it. Make sense?

Since I used to spend much of my discretionary time hunting for my keys, I waged an all-out campaign to formulate a better pattern. Now I have the "keys to success"...literally.

I would lose track of them under stress. Following a stolen car episode, I vowed to get a better pattern established. I won't go into everything I did, but the basic steps would fit most objects.

It involved:

- Setting up a new attitude with accompanying directions to myself about keys. "I enjoy using, not losing keys. I always hook them on my organizer."
- Deciding on a convenient place to keep them. I only have two places: the keys I use daily go on the organizer; the keys I use rarely are all together in one spot in the house.

- Establishing a habit of always putting them back in the same place. Every time I snap the keys onto my purse I feel a sense of control and satisfaction.

The Loose Dewey Decimal System

Reference books (encyclopedias and dictionaries)
Genealogy
Philosophy & Religion
Social Sciences
Pure Science (Botany, Math, Zoology)
Applied Sciences (Health, Medicine, Computer, Construction)
Arts (including gardening)
Literature
Education
Languages
History & Geography (+Travel)

Summary: Chapter 11
Kindergarten Filing In Easy Steps

- *Make your shopping list: You'll need hanging files and frames, file folders (regular and tickler) and something like a file cabinet to put them in.*
- *Establish a simple 4-part, hanging file system with broad categories.*
- *The 4 parts are:*

    Banking/Bill-paying
    Business (for current affairs)
    Investment/Permanent Records
    "Tickler" files.

- *List the contents of the files in pencil, placing the list at the front of the file. Label the folders using nouns and broad categories.*
- *Touch papers only once; TAF it: toss it, act on it, file it or give it away.*
- *Put papers in the back of the file, creating a chronological order.*
- *Keep the file contents and the contents list up to date.*
- *Purge and replace files annually. Store the past 5-7 years file contents in book boxes marked with the year.*
- *Use a computer, money management software and the Internet to make your financial moves easier.*
- *Use a personal planner.*

Twelve

Fine Tuning

Do you feel like "Millennium Man or Woman" with your emergency fund in place, index fund purchased, emotional "tapes" and addictions handled, debt and expenses and organization under control? Then you're ready for fine-tuning your finances.

By now you know that I believe in being very involved with your own money. I have repeatedly urged you to start now.

If you skipped the part where I suggested goal setting, draw a circle on a sheet of paper and divide it into four parts, labeling them *Health*, *Wealth*, *Life Purpose* and *Relationships*.

Write down what you want to have happen in each area. Be very specific and write a target time for when you will have this accomplished.

Select a group of people to support you. It's like killing an elephant. "How's that?" you may ask.

Once a village in the jungle was terrorized by a rogue elephant. The village leader was troubled, and seeing his concern, a small nondescript fellow approached him.

"Do not worry, sir. I killed the elephant."

Dubiously, the leader scanned the unimpressive figure before him and reacted, "You? How did you kill the elephant?"

"With my club, sir," the diminutive fellow responded.

"Your club? How big is your club?" the astonished chief asked.

"Oh, about a hundred and fifty members," was the reply.

Example of Goals:

Health: "Before the year is up, I will be five pounds lighter."

Wealth: "I will have enough money to retire when I am sixty-two years old."

Life Purpose: "I am active as an advocate for children."

Relationships: "I have a happy marriage by the year 2003."

Pick one of the areas…the one that means the most to you. Make one move, no matter how tiny, toward that goal.

For instance:

Health: Call a friend and invite her/him to walk with you or investigate nearby health clubs.

Life Purpose: Call some agencies like "Voices for Children" and ask what their needs are.

Relationships: Evaluate yourself as marriage material. Let appropriate people know your intentions.

Wealth: Make an appointment with your company's benefit representative to discuss your retirement needs or send for a Social Security report of estimated earnings.

One small step will get you moving. Now that you are in motion, let's talk about increasing the amount of money that your investments bring in, and how to custom-tailor your plan for prosperity.

Increasing Your Return

Surprise! It's simple and clear-cut. The return on your money, the amount it is earning for you, increases when you:

Decide how much risk you can tolerate.

Put lots of money in the investment that fits your risk tolerance and is tax-sheltered. Some people have nightmares if the investment they have dips in value, even if it quickly rebounds. They have what we call a low risk tolerance. They are happier with a fixed return, no matter if it's low.

Leave it alone to grow as long as you possibly can.

Asset allocation, deciding where to put your investment money, can account for as much as 94 percent of your future financial gains. There are only five things you can do with your money: give it away, spend it, lend it, invest it and pay your taxes. Asset allocation deals with the part you invest.

Don't Forget Taxation

According to the Washington-based Tax Foundation, the average family's tax bill already is approaching 40 percent of its total income. This exceeds what families spend on food, clothing, shelter and transportation combined. By way of contrast, even the most oppressed of medieval serfs had to give the local lord "only" one-third of their output And since serfs were considered slaves, what does that make us? (We live lots better, of course.)

Be alert to every opportunity to reduce your taxes. Every financial move can be evaluated from a tax angle. Here's an over-achiever to illustrate this concept:

> *"You are being arraigned here today for claiming your cats as dependents," the judge told a defendant, "and treating your losses at the casino as capital losses. How then do you plead to the charge of tax evasion?"*
> *"Guilty, Your Honor."*
> *"What do you have to say before I set your fine?" the judge asked.*
> *"Are fines tax deductible?" asked our hero.*

Well, that was a bit zealous, but paying your fair share means using every legal strategy available to lighten your taxes.

Assets

What are assets? Real assets are:

- Businesses that do not require your presence. (You own them; others manage them.)
- Stocks
- Bonds
- Mutual Funds
- Income-generating real estate
- Notes (IOUs)
- Royalties (from music, scripts, patents, etc.)
- Anything else that has value, produces income or appreciates and has a ready market

How you divide your money between the groups is called asset allocation. To decide that, financial companies offer suggestions or formulas like:

Relatively Conservative (in or near retirement) Put 45 percent of your assets in stocks, 35 percent in bonds or annuities, and 20 percent in money market mutual funds or short term savings accounts.

Moderate (ages 45-65) Stocks, 60 percent, 35 percent in bonds, real estate, or annuities and 5 percent in money market funds.

Aggressive (35-45) 85 percent stocks, 10 percent bonds or annuities, 5 percent money market funds.

Most Aggressive (under 35) Stocks, 95 percent; 5 percent, bonds.

But, wait! There's something you should know about any of these formulas.

Each individual is unique and each formula is only a general guideline. Don't worry about perfection, either.

Yes, all of us need to put our money to work, earning as much as possible. We also want complete safety. A good asset allocation for you reaches a balance between safety and yield that is comfortable for you.

Personalized Asset Allocation

When our sons were in high school, we went on a boat/camping trip to Lake Powell, joined by our pre-teen nephew Chris and one of my sons' friends, Jim, plus the family dogs. Two days into our vacation and many miles from the marina, the boat broke down so badly it wouldn't respond to my handy husband's efforts to start it.

We held a meeting and developed a plan for our rescue. Our son, Kelly, and his friend, Jim, volunteered to hike across the desert and retrieve the pickup. According to the map, Chris, Milt and I could float the boat down one of the lakes' fingers and meet them. Then we could tow the boat to a mechanic on the trailer pulled by the pickup. They set out, with water and my silent prayers, in the cool of the early morning.

   I won't go into every ghastly thing that happened, but can you picture an 11-year-old, and a man and small woman pushing, pulling, and paddling a 16-foot boat down a rapidly shrinking stream to meet the pickup? Soon, we were dragging the boat over sand bars, harnessed like oxen.

   The rapidly rising lake had dislodged swarms of stinging gnats, which were violently attracted to sweaty human bodies. When someone smiled, which wasn't often, you could see gnats embedded between their teeth. We wrapped sweatshirts around our faces in a desperate attempt to protect our bare skin from the voracious insects. They particularly favored me, probably because I was the more perfumed of the group. Or maybe because they instinctively sensed my allergy to their stings.

   When we finally reached the dead end of the finger of the lake, now a trickle, we could see the waiting pickup. Kelly and Jim had made it! However, there was an expanse of loose and bottomless sand stretching between the boat and the trailer hitch on the pickup.

   So, naturally, when the pickup became stuck in the sand, we had to build a road, dragging and rolling slabs of flat rock to form the base. The gnats liked this project even better.

   There were other events, but those were the highlights.

   This is my point: When we finally, after about 12 hours of struggle, did reunite pickup and boat, my husband was mystified and a little disappointed that his little troupe voted unanimously—in my case, hysterically—to spend the night in a motel and have a hot meal.

   What is even more to the point, when we returned to civilization, I told all and sundry about "My Camping Trip in Hell." A friend commented that Kelly must have been on a different trip because he described it as great fun, a big adventure and one of the best ones ever.

What does this have to do with asset allocation? One person's investment hell is another's heaven, and they may be the same investment.

One size does not fit all, so bear in mind the following when you balance your portfolio between more and less risky investments:

- Your own knowledge, skills and background
- Your investment horizon ...how long until you need to use the money invested
- Your tolerance for risk
- Your need for growth

Your Knowledge and Skills

Are you street smart about money? Or are you clueless? Are you confident and interested? Do you understand numbers especially when coupled with dollar signs? Or do you need a helping hand and lots of support in the realm of finances?

If, up until now, you have been clueless, you may need a financial planner. They vary widely in areas of expertise. I've provided a thumbnail sketch of what some of those letters behind their names signify and contact numbers for organizations. Some will tell you about an individual's history, including consumer complaints, disciplinary actions and criminal charges. Some will not.

List Of Financial Advisors And Contacts

CFP, or Certified Financial Planner-Must pass a two-day exam. Three to five years of financial-planning work experience also required. Certified Financial Board of Standards, Phone: (303) 830-7500 Web: http://www.CFP-Board.org

CPA, or Certified Public Accountant-Must have bachelor's degree, pass a national exam and continually keep up with changing tax laws. Should also be a member of the American Institute of Certified Public Accountants, Phone: (888) 777-7077 Web: http://www.aicpa.org

CFA, or Chartered Financial Analyst-Must pass three tests that require expertise in investing. Emphasis is on financial analysis and portfolio management. Must have bachelor's degree and three years of experience in financial sector. Association for Investment Management and Research. Phone: (800) 247-8132 Web: http://www.aimr.org

ChFC or Chartered Financial Consultant-Must have three years of experience in financial services. Must complete a 10-course curriculum that focuses on comprehensive financial planning issues. Society of Financial Service Professionals. Phone: (610) 526-2500. Web: http://www.financialpro.org

CLU or Chartered Life Underwriter-Awarded to life insurance agents. Must complete 10 insurance-related courses. Society of Financial Service Professionals. Phone: (610) 526-2500. Web: http://www.financialpro.org

EA or Enrolled Agent-Must pass a two-day tax exam and background check, both administered by the Internal Revenue Service. Should be a member of the National Association of Enrolled Agents. Phone: (800) 424-4339. Web: http://www.naca.org

PFS or Personal Financial Specialist-Awarded to CPAs who have at least three years of financial planning experience, pass a six-hour financial planning exam and complete 72 hours of continuing education every three years. Must be a member of the American Institute of Certified Public Accountants. Phone: (888) 777-7077. Web: http://www.alcpa.org

RR or registered representative, a stockbroker-Must pass exams administered by the National Association of Securities Dealers and any exams required by the state. Must be licensed by state securities agency and registered with NASD if they buy or sell for clients for compensation. Phone: (800) 289-9999. Web: http://www.nasdr.com

RIA or Registered Investment Adviser-Anyone can become an RIA by registering with the Securities and Exchange Commission, filing a form and paying a fee.

Another way to handle this is to buy mutual funds and invest passively, letting the experts decide when to buy and sell. This saves time, as well.

If you have some special expertise, use it in your portfolio. Maybe you know a lot about the retail business. Utilize it to pick a business to buy or to analyze a company's stock. Don't laugh! You can have a piece (share) of some pretty impressive business for under $100. A lot of those pieces can make you rich.

One of our friends does well in coins and precious metals because of his hobby, which I can't even pronounce, but it means "coin collecting." He even collects profits from the sale of a book he wrote on one kind of coin.

Almost half of our portfolio is in real estate at this time. It's a natural for us. I like to shop for good real estate deals and my husband is a builder, handy with tools for repair jobs.

In thirteen years of renting and managing we've had to deal with only five problems: one new roof, one new furnace, one late rent check, one flood from a neighbor's waterbed and some ants. It's our "investment heaven." Would it be yours?

You can buy shares in Real Estate Investment Trusts (REIT's) which are traded publicly, for more diversity and less active involvement.

Keep investments you understand. Warren Buffett does. My mother loves CD's, low yield and all. She knows exactly what to expect from them and part of the definition of wealth should include "peace of mind." Most Newbies need a higher yield.

Get a professional to help you if you need to for your peace of mind, but still stay involved.

Your Investment Horizon Do you get a mental picture of someone riding or striding toward a setting sun? Well, it's taking the sun a lot longer to sink below the horizon nowadays…about twenty five years longer. People are living longer, more active lives. This creates a need for new money rules.

Senior citizens who assumed they could retire happily on bonds and CDs are finding out otherwise. With 20 years of bill paying ahead of them, they need to put some growth back into the portfolio to maintain their standard of living. They…and you and I…need to continue to invest. Except among the very rich, the good life cannot long be preserved without stocks.

Read *Beating the Street* by Peter Lynch who quips, Gentlemen who prefer bonds don t know what they re missing.

With this in mind, how long should your horizon be…your time before you begin to draw heavily on your investments?

The short answer is "As long as you can stand it." Time is a powerful ally. Put it in stocks or mutual funds featuring stocks, leave it alone to grow, and you'll thank yourself…a lot!

You look so serious, with all this heavy discussion. Take time out for a game.

So, you are responsible for providing at least 56 percent of your own hopefully adequate retirement income. Early re-

The Retirement Game

Test yourself:

What percentage of your pre-retirement income do you think you'll need to live comfortably during retirement?
A 50%   B 60%   C 70-80%   D 90%

At what age should you begin to save seriously for retirement?
A 30   B 40   C 50   D ASAP

If you retire at age 62, your monthly Social Security payment will be about what percent less than if you retire at age 65?
A 10%   B 15%   C 20%   D. 25%

Employer-sponsored plans, such as 401(k)s and 403(b)s, allow employees to build up retirement savings tax-deferred.
A True   B False

For the average retiree, Social Security provides what percentage of the individual's retirement income?
A 74%   B 51%   C 63%   D 44%

Which factor needs to be taken into account when planning for retirement?
A Inflation   B Social Security   C Pensions
D All of the factors

(Answers: C, D, C, True, D, and D)

tirement reduces your income. Let's get on with building your portfolio.

You may also want to consider retiring to a part time job or a different career that appeals to you. More and more people are redefining the "golden years." Even AARP (formerly the American Association of Retired People) dropped the word "Retirement" from its name, retaining the acronym.

Risk

First consider risk. The higher paying investments are riskier, in terms of market risk. Let's look at other kinds of risk, too.

When financial "gooroos" talk about a risky investment, they usually mean market risk.

There are six broad categories of risk:

- *Market Risk* This is the mugger or highwayman variety of risk that openly demands or snatches your purse. It includes such factors as Wall Street hysteria, political changes like wars or elections, and crowd psychology.

    You can measure it by watching the ups and downs of the Standard & Poor's Stock Index, published in the business section of most newspapers. Over long periods of time, ten years or more, you can tolerate these gyrations and make money, if you have the temperament.

- *Inflation risk* When prices rise, the purchasing power of your dollars erodes. Fifteen years of 5 percent inflation will reduce the value of $1,000 to $481. Low-yielding investments, such as savings accounts and certificates of deposit, may not earn enough to beat the climbing cost of living. Inflation also cuts the value of future income on fixed-income investments, such as long-term bonds. Inflation is the sneak thief of risk.

- *Interest-rate risk* Higher borrowing rates make price of existing bonds fall as rates go up, making

their yields unattractive. Stocks of industries whose profits depend partly on interest rates, such as banks, savings and loans and home builders, are also held hostage by this culprit.
- *Economic risk* Slower economic growth can cause investments to fall in price, such as a drop in oil prices or a depression in Detroit or Denver real estate prices.
- *Company-specific risks* Stocks are vulnerable to events that affect only a particular company or industry. International stocks may have all these risk factors plus the fluctuation of currency prices and government instability.
- *Taxes and Costs* Some investments invite taxation. Just when you're on the way to the bank with your dollars, this thief ambushes you and demands a sizable cut. Or maybe it's the unexpected high cost of doing business a certain way, like frenzied buying and selling of positions in the market or a rear-end load (commission).

It only makes sense to diversify among investments with varying degrees of risk.

Market Risk can be minimized with a choice of some investments on the low risk end of the Market Risk spectrum. Bear in mind that, if you can tolerate risky investments to some extent, as in stocks, you have a greater potential return over time, however.

The riskiest investments do not belong in a long-term portfolio. Late Starters can't afford to experiment. Beginners, wouldn't you really rather make money consistently than ride a wild roller coaster with an inevitable wreck at the end of the ride? Profit from the mistakes of others; you can't live long enough to make them all yourself.

Interest-rate risk is minimized when you limit choices of industries that depend partly on interest rates, like mortgages, financial institutions and construction.

Inflation risk hits hard at the so-called safe investments with the lower yield.

Perhaps your CD is earning 6 percent and it's taxed on top of that. Inflation may be hovering around 5 percent. Your investment is melting like a soft serve ice cream cone on a hot day in Gila Bend, Arizona!

A fixed, tax-sheltered annuity grows modestly until you pull it out. Then come taxes, penalties in some cases, and transaction fees.

Your goal is a mix of investments that balances the different kinds of risk. Here's a list of investments arranged in order from lowest *market* risk down to highest risk.

Market Risk Spectrum

Certificates of Deposit, Money Market Funds
Fixed Annuities
Bonds (GNMAs, Government Bonds, Corporate Bonds
Utility Stocks, Convertible Bonds, Preferred Stocks
Real Estate
Income and Growth Stocks
Growth Stocks
Aggressive Growth Stocks
International Stocks
Commodities (Gold, Metals, Currencies), Collectibles
Options, Futures, Penny Stocks

I suppose next riskiest would be throwing money out of a moving vehicle.

Notice the absence of a "mutual fund" or a variable annuity listing. That's because a mutual fund can be comprised of Money Market Securities, stocks bonds or a combination thereof. Someday, I wouldn't be surprised to see a mutual fund for "Beanie Babies." There's even one for so-called "sin industries" (liquor, gambling, tobacco, etc.)

A variable annuity is an insurance to draw on at retirement that has mutual fund choices and tax-shelter advantages, but many rules to follow about when and how you can draw on your money without suffering substantial penalties.

Let's do a two-minute assessment of you, so we can design your asset allocation. Put the following factors in order of importance to you, 1 for most important, 4 for least important:

- Safety of money
- Growth of money
- Guidance/Help in money decisions
- Caring for my family; personal protection in case of disability

Is there a clear-cut winner for you? Nearly all New Lifers, who often get a late start in assuming control of money matters need growth of money.

They are also concerned with safety, because they can't readily make up monetary losses. A good choice for them is a large company stock or mutual fund investing primarily in large companies.

If safety is your number one consideration, choose from the low risk end of the spectrum. Protection of family as a top choice warrants an emphasis on insurance. You say you want both growth and security? Read on.

Don't Pass This Up!

Put as much money as you can in tax-sheltered investments like 403(b)s and 401(k)s. What a good deal! A 403(b) is limited to government or non-profit institutions' employees.

If you put 19% of a $35,000 salary in a 401(k) with a 50% company match on the first 6%, and your investment earns a 10% annual rate, your money will have grown 36% in just one year, according to David Godofskyof Godofsky, Bryan, Pendleton, Swats & McAllister.

There are limits to the amount the government will let you shelter, which you can check on the Tax Shelter chart on page 87.

By the way, if you've wondered about a conversion to a Roth IRA, it's only worthwhile for those in the lowest (15%) tax bracket. The conversion would require you to pay tax now on the income that would have resulted if such amounts had been distributed. (Source: Edelman Financial Services, Inc., Fairfax, Virginia.) Research Roth IRAs on the Internet or ask your accountant about starting one. You want one only if it fits your situation.

In a divorce settlement, the spouse receiving an IRA distribution can roll over the funds into another IRA and avoid penalty. (Source: *Income Tax & Financial Planning Handbook*, 1999 Edition, from TMI Tax Services.)

Growth and Security Combined

Here's an idea for asset allocation for you who are equally concerned with growth and safety:

Put your investments mostly in stocks of the Blue Chip variety or an Index 500 fund. You must be resigned to leaving this money alone for at least ten years, longer if possible. Leave the rest in a money market mutual fund for emergencies. Adjust this asset allocation for your individual preferences and needs.

The stock part plus the tax deferred and tax deductible status gives you a chance for growth with a reasonable amount of safety.

If you buy individual stocks, choose at least five of the sort in the low risk category (See Chapter 7, "What About Stocks?" for pointers.) Over the past 50 years, there have been 16 market corrections of 10% or more, most of them Fed-induced. The sectors that have done best during those market setbacks include:

- Energy
- Telecommunications
- Health Care*Utilities.

Computer technologies have not constituted a sector for the second half of the century, but have performed well in recent corrections.

Those willing to take on the added market risk of individual stocks can pick among these sectors. Choose a company that has a commanding share of their sector, like AT&T or Microsoft.

If you want more diversity, and desire less company specific risk, you can buy Sector-based equity portfolios or S&P Depositary Receipts (SPDRs). They are packages of stocks of companies in specific sectors. Most trade on the American Stock Exchange.

Instead of buying four or five individual stocks in a promising sector, you can allocate 60% to this type of security and gain exposure to entire sectors. Leading choices...

- Energy Select Sector SPDRs Fund (More than 30 energy related stocks)
- Technology Select Sector SPDRs Fund (100 high-technology stocks from S&P 500)

Keep your costs down by using discount brokers, buying directly from the company (See "DRIPS," page 123) or by getting a low cost index fund. (See "No-Load Index Funds," page 67).

Your biggest risk is Market Risk, which you have minimized with the choice of solid company stock and by committing to a longer time period of investment.

If you are comfortable with stocks and stock market mutual funds then put as much money as you can do without. Leave it alone to grow for at least 7-10 years.

Once you have maxed out the limits of the tax shelters you can establish taxable accounts with low turnover (Keep those costs down!) or invest in variable annuities which have a tax deferred status and offer choices in different mutual funds. Here again, go for the Blue Chip or slightly riskier stocks.

Put a bunch in this allocation. If you are equally concerned with growth and safety, invest 50% or more.

For the rest of the allocation, divide between Bonds, Money Markets and CD's.

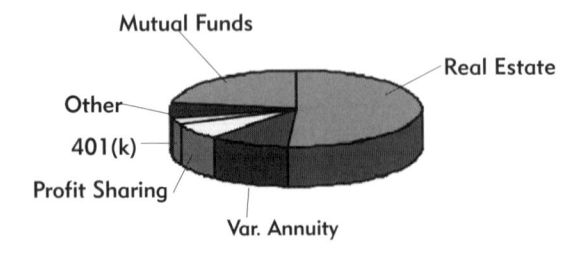

Asset allocation in one account

Stock Categories

(listed in order of market risk, starting with the LOWEST risk first)

An individual stock represents a share of ownership-or equity-in a corporation. Because of their importance in today's portfolios, I've devoted an entire chapter to them, "What About Stocks?" so this discussion is limited to risk.

- *Blue-Chip Stocks* are stocks of seasoned companies. Established companies that have paid regular dividends in both good and bad years are considered blue chips (Texas Instruments, Federal Express Corp., and Ford Motor Company, for example.) Large company stocks have an annual return of 12.97% 1970-1997.
- *Income Stocks* tend to be in stable service industries, such as telecommunications and utilities. Like blue-chips, they are considered a low-risk investment compared with other stocks.
- *Growth Stocks* are typically in younger or smaller companies. They have the potential to rise or fall significantly in market value over a relatively short period of time (one to five years). They also have greater potential for price appreciation.
- *Small-Company Stocks* are considered highly speculative because the companies are in the early stages of growth or are in very young industries that have little or no track record. Some of the biotechnology stocks are considered speculative, for example. These investments also have the greatest potential for price appreciation IF and when the marketplace recognizes their worth. Small com-

pany stocks have an annual return of 13.28% 1970-1997.

See the graph, "Stocks Have Outpaced other Investments" below.

Stocks have outperformed other investments

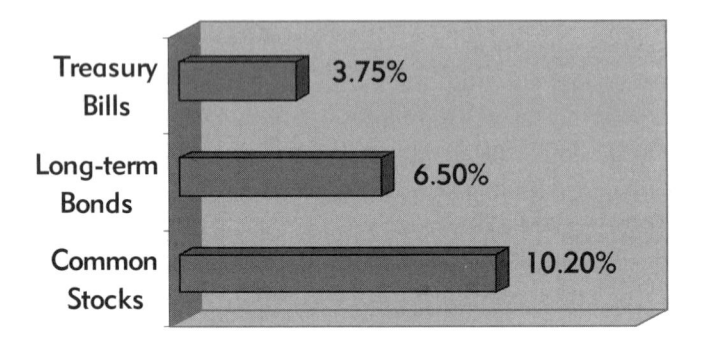

- Treasury Bills: 3.75%
- Long-term Bonds: 6.50%
- Common Stocks: 10.20%

Average annual returns from 1926 through 1992

Bonds

What is a bond? A bond is an IOU.

Just like you do when you forget your lunch money and borrow it from someone, large organizations like corporations, the federal government, and state or local governments all need to borrow money occasionally.

They need so much money that they have to agree to pay back the amount they borrowed , plus a little extra in the form of a fee (interest) for the privilege of borrowing the money.

The bonds are sold to the public in set increments, normally in the neighborhood of $1,000. You, the lender, get a piece of paper that says how much was lent, the agreed-upon interest rate, how often interest will be paid, and the term of the loan (how long they'll keep your money).

There are four basic kinds of bonds, all defined by who needs the money.

- The first are bonds sold by the U.S. government and their agencies.
- The second are bonds sold by corporations.
- The third type of bonds are those sold by state and local governments.
- The last type of bond is sold by foreign governments.

Bonds don't have much market risk, with the exception of foreign or state bonds with dubious management, but they do vary according to interest rates.

I will confine my discussion of them to three safe bonds that are relatively easy to buy: EE Savings Bonds, Zero-Coupon Bonds, and Treasury Issues.

EE Savings Bonds They need less maintenance than dandelions. Stash them someplace fireproof and that's it. You receive whatever interest it has made when you cash in the bond for its full face value.

- Other attributes:
- You can buy in for as little as $25
- They are issued and backed by the federal government. Safe!
- You pay no commissions or fees.
- The government replaces them free if they're lost, stolen, or eaten by sharks.
- They provide tax benefits. All interest is exempt from state and local taxes.

- They're never worth less than you pay for them; their prices don't vary inversely with interest rates (unlike other bonds.)

Zero-Coupon Bonds Nothing beats them for predictability. You know exactly how much you'll come into when the bond reaches maturity. Make sure you won't need the money before the bond's maturity; they are about three times as volatile as other bonds. A one-point rise in interest rates can create a double-digit loss if you're forced to sell early.

If you don't mind tying up your money in return for a predictable return, you risk-averse investors may like them. Bonds have had an annual return of 9.01 percent, 1970-1997.

U.S. Treasury Issues Uncle Sam also offers three virtually risk-free securities besides EE bonds, Treasury bills, bonds and notes. They pay competitive rates, provide tax benefits, need no research and are as secure as Fort Knox.

Your Personal Money Profile

You can depend on the following to support you in style, if you have a plan and take action on it:

- Personal and Business Assets
- Employment Benefits
- Insurance plans
- Government programs

Take time to answer some questions about each category. It will summarize your current situation.

PERSONAL AND BUSINESS ASSETS

List assets available to produce income.

Savings $ _____
Cds $ _____
Money Market Funds $ _____
Stocks $ _____
Bonds $ _____
Mutual Funds $ _____
Other Available Assets
(Cash value) $ _____

Total Assets $ _____

EMPLOYMENT BENEFITS

Insurance:
    Life $ _____
    Health $ _____
    Disability $ _____
    Profit Sharing $ _____
    Other $ _____

INCOME HISTORY

Employment
    Current Year $ _____
    Last Year $ _____
    Bonus $ _____
    Investment $ _____
    Other $ _____

INSURANCE PLANS (Personal)
    Life
    Auto
    Liability
    Disability
    Health

Dental
Vision
Other

GOVERNMENT PROGRAMS
SSD
SS /PERA
SSD
SS/PERA

Are you eligible for benefits? How much?

How Much Is Enough?

How much do you have to save each month to have enough money to retire?

The simple answer is as much as you can possibly invest, because you're making up for lost time.

A new Web calculator offers better estimates than you've probably ever had before. There are no guarantees, but you should at least test this service at Financial Engines (www.financialengines.com) against any saving target you're using now.

What makes this calculator different is that it figures in the amount of risk you've taken on.

When I fully realized the importance of growing our money, we started living on one income and investing the other one. We didn't do it forever, and it paid off...literally!

Summary—Chapter 12
Fine Tuning Features

- *Specify your goals and your risk tolerance..*
- *Choose appropriate investments and stick with them.*
- *Use Tax Sheltered investments to the max,*
- *investing in non-qualified plans last.*
- *Put your plan into motion.*

Thirteen

Summing Up

...If You Don't Have Time To Read Anything Else...

Life is a checkerboard and the player opposite you is time. "If you hesitate before moving, or neglect to move promptly, your men will be wiped off the board by time. You are playing against a partner who will not tolerate indecision.

So ends Napoleon Hill's classic, *Think and Grow Rich*.

The decision you must make is "To be or not to be...wealthy and secure."

If you choose "To be," your family and community will thank you, because they will benefit.

To Be Wealthy and Secure:

- Define your goals and values.

- Get your personal act together.
- Reduce your spending and debt.
- Increase your investments.
- Guard against financial disasters.

You will either take these steps or, by default, choose not "to be." Remember, just sitting on a rock thinking prosperous thoughts is not enough to ensure your wealth and security.

Aggressive Strategies For Wealth-Building

Intelligence and "guts" are keys to success with money. Use your capacity for risk-taking to be an entrepreneur if that's your calling. The self-made millionaires have done it that way...often in "dull-normal businesses."

"Some Advice to Entrepreneurs" follows this chapter. Children are great entrepreneurs because they don't worry themselves out of acting on an idea.

Our younger son, Dan, decided when he was in Second Grade, that he wanted to learn to play a bugle.

We told him to wait until he was the proper age, as advised by the music teachers we consulted.

He sent away for seeds to sell door-to-door. The top prize was a bugle. You had to sell a *lot* of seeds to earn it. We were living in the mountains four miles from Boulder, Colorado and our nearest neighbors were almost a mile away.

Dan walked to all the neighbors and made his sales pitch.

Imagine an eight year old appearing on your door step after walking miles, clutching a picture of "his" bugle. He was an irresistible force. He saw no possibility but success. The rest of the story? After his bugle arrived, we arranged lessons.

Don't confuse risk-taking and gambling. If you don't know the difference, please read "What About Stocks?" and "The Dirty Dozen of Finance."

You can make up for some lost time by putting your investment dollars to work for you in America's businesses...in stock.

Be a "buy-and-hold" investor. Following the market timing suggestions of the nation's leading brokerage firms resulted in zero value added to the portfolio over the last five years. (Source: Bill Valentine, CFA of Valentine Ventures).

Before you buy an individual stock, answer three questions:

- Is this a high-quality company I'd love to own a piece of?
- Is the price right to buy it now?
- Are individual stocks right for me?

If not, mutual funds offer a diversified, easy, time-efficient, lucrative way to invest. You'll find instructions on picking and buying mutual funds in Chapter 4, "Newbies." If you don't own a home, buy one. It is one of the few good reasons to go into debt...but not too far!

These are all part of your strategies for creating and keeping a wealth building program.

Debt and Spending

A technical term financial pundits like to use for overspending is "stinky." It reeks. Live below your means.

Paying off a credit card that has a 17% interest rate is equivalent to earning 17% on an investment...after taxes!

You can actually "earn" more by paying off a debt, or cutting back on spending than you can by saving and investing.

The best strategy is to do all four...that's how late starters can make up for some lost time. You create financial miracles when you reduce debt, cut spending, increase savings and put every dollar possible to work investing.

If you can't pay off your high-rate debt immediately, take steps to reduce the interest rate you pay. You can apply for a low-interest-rate card or negotiate a lower rate through your current card issuers Remember the word "negotiate." You can negotiate or bargain for the price of everything from hamburger (or tofu) to C.D. rates.

See Chapter 8, "Debt: When Your Outgo Exceeds Your Income'" for specific strategies, and for the one time it doesn't make sense to kill your debt.

Finance appreciating assets (e.g. real estate, equities) only. Wait until you can afford the other "stuff" without borrowing.

Security and Bargains

Start contributing to a tax-favored retirement savings plan.

If you're lucky enough to work for a company that offers a retirement savings plan like a 401(k), you should take advantage of it.

Many employers will match a portion of the amount you put into such a plan. That means the company will contribute a set amount...say, fifty cents...for every dollar you contribute, up to a specified dollar amount. That's an immediate 50% return on your money. (In fact, if your company offers such a fabulous matching deal, you should probably contribute to the plan even before paying off your credit card debt.

If you are self-employed, start your own SEP-IRA.

Plan ahead for a longer work life, expect smaller public benefits and save more for your retirement.

Reduce all Your Expenses, Especially Taxes

Well, there are a few expenses that pay you more than they cost you, namely education and good professional advice or services. Most personal possessions are never worth as much as you expect, and you're unlikely to sell them.

A tax professional could steer you to tax saving strategies like:

- Parent/Child Exclusion: The transfer of real property between parents and children can be excluded from reappraisal for property tax purposes. Property Tax Postponement Program (CA): One of several options for seniors on limited incomes. This program allows homeowners to postpone payment of part or all of the property taxes on their residence. (Other benefits for seniors and disabled are Reappraisal Exclusions. Call your County Assessor for more information.)
- Like-Kind Exchanges: This allows the sale of income-producing property to go untaxed if another of "like kind" is purchased.
- Capital Gains Tax Exclusion: If you have lived in your home for the last two years, you can sell the home and take $250,000 of gain without capital gains taxation ($500,000 for married home sellers who file jointly). Home sellers can make use of this rule as often as every two years.

Best of all, if you move into your Like-Kind Exchange rental unit, making it your primary residence, it becomes eligible for the Capital Gains Exclusion. If you don't sell for two years, you don't pay capital gains on either your rental unit or your original primary residence.

You can save on most items by comparison shopping. Think how much you save if you don't buy at all. Don't trade financial independence, freedom and power for a new car or carpet.

Financial Ruin: Avoid It

Financial disasters can come at us from outside and inside ourselves.

Avoid the outside onslaught by providing appropriate protection with insurance and an emergency fund. Jimmy Buffett sings: "Spendin' money! Makes a rainy day turn sunny!" Listen to Jimmy.

Heed the warnings of Chapters 3 and 9, "The Financial Dirty Dozen" and "Dealing with ETs (Emotional Troubles), if your own worst financial enemy is yourself. Then it's an "inside job." Ask for help if you need it.

Stay resume' ready by making your business or job a keeper. Maybe your job's not a keeper, if it offers no benefits. Even the high school kids carrying out groceries have insurance, working for unionized grocery stores.

A general insurance guide is in Chapter 4, "Newbies," but it is no substitute for an informed, honest insurance agent.

Plan ahead for big money events like college expenses and responsibilities for parents and build up that emergency fund!

Get It All Together

Although it's been said that "happiness is having a caring, communicative family...in a distant city," I urge you to strengthen family ties. It may be an extended family, but you will benefit financially and other ways. People need people.

I'm not talking about getting financial first aid from your relatives, either. I'm referring to synergy, the power that comes from pooling energy and resources.

Change bad habits, whether they are physical or mental; weed them out. Carefully replace them with more productive ones.

Read Chapter 10, "Home on the Range (Encouraging Words)" if you get discouraged at your lack of "instant perfection."

Your life is a river and a few little fingers of water meandering off the main course don't change the flow of the main stream; it's the general direction you're going that counts.

You can make up for lost time and missed opportunities by following the low risk, high-powered strategies in this money book. The strategies are summarized at the end of every chapter.

These strategies work, work for everyone and work all the time. You'll get immediate pay-off in pride, power, and prosperity. It starts with your decision to be friends with your money.

There's still the "frog problem," described by Mark L. Feldman and Michael F. Spratt in *Five Frogs on a Log* (Harper Business):

> *Five frogs are sitting on a log. Four decide to jump off. How many are left?*
>
> Answer: Five.
>
> *Why? Because there's a difference between deciding and doing.*

Appendix A

Business Start-Up Advice

(Source: Mildred Leet, "Trickle Up Program" grants to entrepreneurs)

- Talk to as many entrepreneurs as possible.
- Questions to ask:
    - ❑ What kind of drive and time were required to start your business?
    - ❑ How did you keep the stress from tearing apart your family?
    - ❑ What legal issues do entrepreneurs have to worry about when starting out?
    - ❑ Where is the best place to operate the kind of business I want to start?
    - ❑ How much money will I need in my first year?
- Write a business plan that makes sense.
- Ask yourself:
    - ❑ How does my business fit into the market place?

❏ How is my business going to compete with similar businesses?

❏ How is my business going to distinguish itself from similar businesses?

- Include: Business profile, Marketing Profile, Financial Profile and Management Profile.
- Be as stingy as possible with your capital.
- Learn to do your own books. *Quicken* and *QuickBooks* are helpful software packages.
- Be prepared for a sudden rush of business.

Appendix B

"Crib Notes" For Comparing Investments

EE Savings Bonds: Need less maintenance than Old Faithful. Can't be called before maturity. Backed by Federal Government. Interest exempt from state and local taxes. Bonds held less than 5 years pay reduced interest but rise to 6%. Bonds bought after 1989 pay federal tax-free interest if used for your child's college tuition.

CDs: Not liquid. Time varies between 7 days and 7 years. Taxed. Beware of shaky institutions and misleading quotes.

Money Market Mutual Fund: Offers yield, liquidity and safety. Pays 1.5% to 2% more than bank money market funds. You can invest in a fund that buys only muni-bonds issued by your state with earnings triply exempt...from local, state and federal taxes.

Bank Money Market Account: You must maintain minimum balance. Federally insured.

Treasury Bills, Bonds and Notes: Yield is less than CDs. Exempt from local and state taxes.

Ginnie Mae Certificates: Pools of home mortgages offer convenience and high yield with low risk; backed by Government National Mortgage Association. Minimum for single Ginnie Mae, $25,000; Additional, $5,000. Older Ginnie Maes, $10,000. Never a certain yield; value rises and falls like other bond prices. *Exercise caution during high interest rates.*

Stock Mutual Funds: Professional management and diversification; liquidity, variety, minimal paper work, low minimums. Best investment over time, but can drop short term, e.g. 20.9% in 1987.

Blue-Chip Stocks: Must do your own diversification; they take time to grow, subject to fluctuation. Taxed. One of best yields.

Zero Coupon Bonds: Taxed. Can be volatile. Beware of callable bonds. Buy AAA rated. STRIPS are safest.

Cash Value Insurance: Tax-deferred earnings. Guaranteed minimum rate of return, usually 4% (Single Premium Whole Life or Adjustable Life.) Invest only with company that has $1 billion in assets and an A+ rating from A.M. Best.

(Variable: More like a mutual fund with some insurance.)

Appendix C

Toll-Free Numbers

Credit Reports
- Experian 888-397-3742

Debt
- Consumer Counseling 888-493-8113
- Federal Trade Commission 887-FTC-HELP
- National Foundation for Consumer Credit 800-284-1723
- Student Loans 4FED-AID

DRIPs
- General Electric 786-2543
- Johnson & Johnson 524-3896
- McDonald's Corp 621-7825
- Wm. Wrigley Jr. Co. 824-9681

Index Funds (800)
- T. Rowe Price Total Market (POMEX) 541-8803
- Vanguard Total Stock Market (VTSMX) 871-3879
- (Also see Index Funds)

Mutual Fund Families with low minimums (800)
- Strong Funds 368-1030
- TIAA-CREF Funds 223-1200.

Personal Organizers (800)
- Day Runner Inc. 635-5544
- Day-Timers Inc 225-5005
- Franklin Covey Co. 269-1812

Software, Money Management (800)
- Quicken (Intuit) 433-8810

Appendix D

Web site URLs

Books
- amazon.com
- barnesandnoble.com

Credit
- bankrate.com
- ramresearch.com
- getsmartinc.com
- experian.com

Computer Skills
- iteachyou (San Diego Area free classes)
- jobhuntersbible..com

Debt
- insiderreports.com
- nfcc.org (National Foundation for Consumer Credit.)
- ftc.gov (Federal Trade Commission)

DRIPS (Dividend Reinvestment Plans)
- investorguide.com/DRIPS

Education Cost Calculator
- cunamutual.com/realwrld/educcalc.htm

Gamblers Anonymous
- gamblersanonymous.org

Mortgages, Home
- bankrate.com
- hsh.com

Mutual Funds
- indexfundsonline.com
- morningstar.com

Real Estate
- fanniemae.com
- freddiemac.com

Retirement
- financialengines.com (calculator)
- globe-pequot.com (publisher, *Where to Retire*)

Timeshares
- tug2.net
- tstoday.com

Search Engines
- (See 72-73.)

Stocks
- quicken.com
- snap.com
- stocksite.com/index.ss
- thestreet.com

- fool.com

Small Business Administration
- sba.gov

Tornadoes
- Tornadoproject.com

Treasury Bills
- savingsbonds.com
- publicdebt.treas.gov (Choose TreasuryDirect.)

Glossary[1]

Asset Allocation What investments your money is in and in what proportion, e.g., you might have half your investments in stocks and half in bonds (although I hope you don't). I love to see assets shown in the shape of a pie. Yum!

Assets Whatever puts money in your pocket (earns for you). No, your Mercedes convertible is not an asset, unless you've started an upscale taxi service with it.

Automatic Investment Plan A wonderful deal where you agree to have a certain amount of money taken out of your checking account every month and placed in the investment of your choice, maybe an Index fund. Many advantages.

Bankruptcy Cancels certain kinds of debt but pummels your credit rating, is expensive, means loss of independence, and feels bad. On the plus side, you get to start over, hopefully, and handle finances differently.

---

[1] This is meant to be a very friendly list of terms, defined simply. If I skipped something or a definition was no help to you, let me know. Coleen

Beating the Dow The Dow means the Dow Jones Industrial Average (DJIA). It's an average of about 30 blue chip stocks that people watch to see how the market is doing. If your investments do better than that average, you're "beating the Dow". These 30 stocks are mostly "Industrials" (See definition.)

Blue Chip Stocks Common stocks of nationally known companies that have a long record of profit and good management, like IBM or General Electric.

Bonds IOU from a company or institution. You loan them money, they pay interest a specified times and promise to pay the whole sum back at maturity. There are different kinds of bonds, but that's about enough for now.

Broker A person who is a middleman (or woman) between you, the buyer, and the insurance policy, real estate or investment you are buying. They buy it for you and get money, a commission, for the service. Note: This service costs you, one way or another.

CD's Certificates of Deposit. A debt that pays interest to you. Banks sell them. (See "Fine Tuning" and "Easy Investments" for advantages and disadvantages.)

Chapter 7, 11, and 13 Different kinds of bankruptcy. Chapter 7 cancels debt; Chapter 11 holds off creditors while debtor reorganizes finances; Chapter 13 establishes a court-sanctioned repayment schedule usually over 3 to 5 years. See a credit counselor for details.

COBRA Not a snake. Health insurance that you can get to continue coverage temporarily after your health insurance through your job or other plan is terminated. It means Consolidated Omnibus Budget Reconciliation Act, as if you care.

Glossary

Consolidation of Debt Bringing together all your debts and working out a plan for payment. See a credit counseling service for help on this one.

CCCS One of the credit counseling services you can see about your debt problems. The initials stand for Consumer Credit Counseling Services

Closed-End Funds Most mutual funds are "open-end"; closed-end funds have a fixed number of shares. Stick to open-end funds unless you can't find one doing a good job at whatever it is you're interested in purchasing.

Day trading Buying and selling your assets, usually stocks, in the space of one day. I'm so against this for most people, indeed for about 99% of the human race!

DRIPS Stock sold directly to you from a company, like Coca-Cola or McDonald's. This saves you a commission. Not every company has one of these "Dividend Reinvestment Plans," but you can ask.

Discount brokers Brokers (salespeople) who charge less, and don't give advice. They're supposed to just take your order for a stock or whatever.

Dollar Cost Averaging One of the advantages of an automatic investment plan. You invest a fixed amount of dollars in securities at set intervals. This way you automatically buy more shares when the price is low and less when it's high. How clever of you!

Dow Dividend Approach A way of choosing stocks, described in detail in Chapter 7, "What About Stocks?"

Entrepreneurs Someone who organizes and directs a business or project, assuming the risk for the sake of the profit.

What would we do without these brave, hardy individuals, our small business owners? I love the stories of someone starting in a garage and now owning the town, so to speak.

Garnishment Having your wages attached to pay your debt. You don't want this, and yes, they *can* do that.

Equity Ownership, stocks, the amount of your home that you, not the mortgage company owns. Bonds are different, that's more like a loan you're making.

Equity Line of Credit A certain amount of money you can borrow based on your home ownership. It's worse than a credit card, in that you can lose your home if you don't pay, but it otherwise functions like one.

Equity Loan You take out another loan, with higher interest than your mortgage, to get money. The interest is tax-deductible.

Index In finance, an index is a composite or mixture often expressed as a percentage, that shows ups and downs of markets, prices or the economy.

Index funds A mutual fund that invests in the stocks followed by a particular index. For example, the S&P 500 Fund invests in 500 widely held common stocks in industrial, transportation, financial and utilities. It is flexible, not always exactly in the same sectors in the same weight, following the index. There are other indexes that have mutual funds following them.

Industrials Companies that produce goods and services that are not utility, transportation or financial companies.

IPO Initial public offering. When a company offers its stock to the public for purchase.

IRA Individual retirement account is a personal, tax-deferred retirement account that an employed person can set up with a deposit limited to $2000 a year. There are other tax shelters available. Check them all out!

Low Minimum Mutual Funds Mutual fund folks insist on an investor putting in a certain amount of money at first, called a "minimum" investment. They will sometimes waive the minimum if you agree to an automatic investment plan. The lowest cost I know of is $50 a month, but there used to be $25 ones. Let me know if you find one.

Market timing The practice of trying to guess when to buy and sell stocks for a maximum profit. The investors I'm most impressed with, like Warren Buffett, look for bargains, but don't buy and sell a lot or try the guesswork. Hint: Every time you buy and sell, it costs you. Can you tell I'm biased?

Mutual Funds A professionally managed collection of assets like stocks, bonds and real estate. If you get "no-load," it costs you very little to invest. I've written a lot about mutual funds; read the book!

PMI Private Mortgage Insurance. Reminds me of PMS, don't buy it unless compelled by the lender. Then, get rid of it as soon as their conditions allow. It protects the lender. What it does for you is add to the cost of the home.

Point When you buy a home and take out a mortgage to help you pay for it, they charge you points. A point is 1% of the loan amount. In general, the more points you pay, the lower the interest rate. Points are also tax-deductible.

While we're on the subject, ever wonder why some ads trumpet 7.5% interest rates for a mortgage then mention an 8 percent annual percentage rate right next to it? Lenders are required by the Truth in Lending Act to include points when representing interest rates. I like to compare APR's.

Realtor Real estate agent. First-time home buyers must use one, preferably a full-time agent.

REITs (Pronounced "reet"s.) Function essentially as mutual funds for real estate. It's like buying real estate without a real lot of money. You put money into a fund that buys and manages properties and mortgages, producing income by renting or selling them.

Roth IRA It's a tax shelter that you need to talk to your accountant about. One difference from a regular IRA is that you, in some cases, don't owe a 10% penalty and income taxes on withdrawals.

Search Engine Locations on the Internet where you go to find the information you want. Here's an example: I sign on but I don't know how to find out about mortgages. I type in hotbot (or altavista or yahoo or excite or...) and I'm shown a site where I can type in "mortgages" where it says, "Search." It will then list some places, with descriptions, to go for that information on the Net.

URL Universal Resource Locator. An address typed into a Web browser to locate an Internet resource, kind of like you address a letter. Instead of streets and ZIP codes, the address looks something like: http://www.whitehouse.gov or http://www.newbies-moneyguide.com.

What's a browser? It's software that lets you view pages. Most popular ones are Netscape and Internet Explorer. That's enough cyberspeak for one day! Take Gini Pedersen's class at the San Diego Community College of Continuing Education on "Intro to the Internet." It's free and worth the trip to San Diego, no matter where you live.

Index

A.M. Best, 133, 236
AAII Journal., 117, 119
Abentrod, Susan, 136
Accountant, 48, 50, 59, 80, 131, 150, 206, 214, 248
Allen, Ted, 122
Allstate, 133
Amazon.com, 136, 239
Arizona State University, 29
Asset allocation, 82, 115, 201, 202, 203-05, 213, 214, 216, 243
assets, 66, 80, 108, 117, 129, 170, 202-03, 220-21, 228, 243
Autobiography in Five Short Chapters, 178
Automatic investing, 63
Avoiding Big Money Blunders, 148

Barron's Dictionary of Financial and Investment Terms., 15
Beating the Dow, 121
Beating the Street, 120, 208
Better Business Bureaus, 138
Big Hat, No Cattle, 22
Big three of personal planners, 191
Bilker, Scott, 136
Blue chip stocks, 114, 214, 216, 217, 244
Bolles, Richard Nelson, 147
Bonds, 66, 68, 80, 81, 82, 89, 115, 116, 120, 129, 168, 202, 203, 208, 210, 212, 216, 218-20, 235, 236, 243, 244, 246, 247
Bottom Line/Personal, 129
Brobeck, Stephen, 92
Brokers, 59, 81, 122, 123, 156, 157, 158, 159, 161, 167, 168, 215, 245
Buffet, Warren, 108, 117, 118-19, 120, 156, 171, 208, 247
Buffettology, 119
Burns, David D., 38
Business start-up advice, 233-34

California Society of CPAs, 1962
Calvin and Hobbes, 157
CANSLIM., 119-20
Capozzi, John, 130
Cds (certificates of deposit), 82, 168, 208, 210, 212, 235, 236
Checklist, Financial Security, 81
Churning, 157-8
COBRA, 71 72, 244
Commonwealth Energy, 132
Consolidation of debt, 128, 245
Consumer Credit Counseling Service, 128, 134, 143, 245
Consumer Reports, 133, 141
Covey, Stephen, 57
Credit bureaus,128, 166
Credit Cards, 62, 85, 86, 92, 128, 134, 136, 138, 139, 140, 141, 142, 144, 148, 149, 164, 166, 188, 227, 246
Credit report, 141, 142, 237

249

DALBAR study, 63
Danko, William, See *Millionaire Next Door*
Dappen, Andy, 148
Day Runner Inc.,190, 191, 238
Day-Timers Inc., 190, 191, 238
Daytrading, 115, 162-63, 245
DeAngelis, Barbara, 45
Debt, 47, 62, 78, 94, 101, 127-51, 164, 227-28, 237, 239, 245, 246
DINS couples, 23
Dirty Dozen of Finance list, 154
Discerning Traveler, The, 164
Discount brokers, 159, 162, 215, 245
Dividend Reinvestment Plans (DRIPS), 123-24, 237, 240, 245
Divorce, 19, 20, 23-24, 34, 69, 71-72, 77, 139, 214
Dolan, Daria, 55
Dollar cost averaging,62, 67, 90, 114, 245
Dow Dividend Approach, 121-21, 245
Duke University, 58

Earnings, increasing, 46
Easiest Way to Get Rich chart, 49
Easy Investments compared: 235-36
Edelman Financial Services, 214
Eemergency fund, 27, 55, 69, 92, 230
Entrepreneurs, Advice to, 233
Exceptions to Keep Forever, 84-85
Expenses, Reducing, 128-29, 229-30; see also Chapter 8
Experian (formerly TRW), 142, 166

Federal Trade Commission, 128
Feeling Good: The New Mood Therapy, 38
Filing, Level A, 184-85
Filing, Level Z, 185-90
Financial Advisors, 137, 205-07
Financial Ruin, Avoiding, 230
Five Frogs on a Log, 231
Focus funds, 116

401(k) Guide, 87
Franklin Covey Co, 190, 191, 238
Franklin Quest Co,, See Franklin Covey Co.
Freedman, Mitchell, 162
Friends, 51

Gamblers Anonymous, 174, 240
Gambling., 41, 173, 174, 227
Garnishment (of wages), 144, 246
Gary. Sally, 129
GEICO, 132
Get A Financial Life (Kobliner)., 136
Get Rich Quick Syndrome, 154-57
Glickstein, David and Linda, 164
Goals, 84, 86-94, 111, 124, 161, 200-01, 235
Godofsky, David, 214
Good Life, 24
Gray, John, 20
Green Mountain Energy, 132

Henry, Tom, 156
Hill, Napoleon, 225
Home, 73-74, 128, 141, 142, 144-45, 227, 229, 246
Home defects, 61, 73-74
Home equity, 128, 142-43
Home equity line of credit, 142
How To Make Money in Stocks, 119
Howells, John, 60

Ibbotson Associates, 88
If Time is Money, No Wonder I'm Not Rich, 168
Income Tax & Financial Planning Handbook, 214
Index funds, 66, 67, 69, 79, 80, 81, 83, 159, 214, 237, 246
Inflation, 50, 53, 63, 69, 82, 92, 118, 210, 212
Insurance, 24, 47, 53, 56, 59, 69, 70, 71, 72, 78, 82, 85, 93, 132, 133, 138, 148, 206, 213, 230, 244, 247
insurance, Medigap, 70

Index 251

Internet, 72, 73, 248; See also Appendix D and Search Engines
Inventory, Financial 84, 85
Investing, 42, 62-63, 79-84, 103; See also Chapters 7 and 12)
Investment Clubs, 121
Investment horizon, 91, 124, 205, 208
IRA, 83, 87, 137, 144, 214, 248; See also Tax Shelters
Irwin, Robert, 74

Job, 57-58, 90, 146-47
Job protection, 57

Kelley Blue Book, 141
Kiyosaki, Robert, 129
Kobliner, Beth, 136
Kubler-Ross, Dr. Elisabeth, 35
L
Lady Bountiful syndrome, 172
Lawrence, D.H., 172
Leet, Mildred, 233
Level A, 225, 227
Level Z, 225
Life Strategies: Doing What Works, Doing What Matters., 38
Lifestyle and Relationships, 19
Lloans, 141-42
Long Term Care Insurance, 71
Loose Dewey Decimal System, 194, 196
lottery, 155
Louv, Richard, 53
Low Minimum mutual funds, 247
Lynch, Peter, 117, 120, 208

Managing Your Money, 193
Markese, John, 137
Market Risk Spectrum, 211
Market Timing, 156, 227, 247
Maverick, Pappy, 26
McGraw, Phillip Dr., 38
Memorial societies, 70
Men are from Mars, Women Are from Venus, 20

Microsoft Money 193
Millionaire Next Door, The, 22, 102
Money Game, 13, 20, 25
Money manifestation of ETs, 46
Money Profile, 220
Money Trap, The, 61
Moody's Investors Service, 133
Morgan, JP, 115
Morningstar, 51, 65, 68, 240
Mortgages, 62, 132, 136, 138, 142, 144-45, 247
Motley Fool, 121
Mutual Funds, 51, 59, 62, 65-68, 73, 79, 80, 81, 83, 91, 106, 107, 113, 115, 116, 158, 168, 202, 207, 212, 216, 227, 236, 240, 245, 246, 24779, 272, 294

Name It, Claim It, Tame It, 38, 42
National Foundation for Consumer Credit, 128
Nelson, Portia, 178
New Lifer, 77-95
Newbies' One-Paragraph Guide, 47
Newhart, Stephanie Vanderkellen, 37
No-load, 51, 66, 67, 79, 80, 83, 90, 24780
North American Securities Administrators, 161

O'Higgins, Michael, 120
O'Neil, William, 168
Oprah Winfrey Show, 38
Organizer, personal, 191, 238

Penny Pincher, 129-30
Perry, Ann, 164
Personal organizers (See organizers, personal)
Plastic Prison, 164-66; see also Credit cards
Ponzi schemes, 130-37
Pop psychology";, 43
possibility thinking, 131
Power of Attorney, 70
Prenuptial agreements, 16

Principal Financial Group, 29

Quicken, 85, 92, 123, 193, 234, 238

Real Estate, 61-62, 145, 163, 203, 207, 212, 228, 240, 248

Real Estate Investment Trusts (REITs), 208, 248

Real Moments, 45

Regional Occupational Program (ROP), 57

Retirement, 36, 52-54, 58, 60, 61- 107, 193, 203, 209, 213, 228, 240

Retirement Game, 209

Rich Dad, Poor Dad (Kiyosaki), 129

Risk, 81, 82, 90, 115, 201, 210-13, 215, 216, 217-19, 227

Roaring 2000's (Dent), 91

Rocking Horse Winner, The (Lawrence), 172

Roth IRA, 137, 144, 214, 248

Rule of 72, 91

S&P 500, 63, 67, 80, 81, 107, 135, 246

S&P Depositary Receipts (SPDRs), 215

San Diego Career Center, 57

San Diego's Deals & Steals (Gary), 129

SCORE, 146

Search Engines, 72-73, 248

Select Funds, 116

Serns, Diane, 58

Seven Habits of Highly Effective People, 57

Shaw, George Bernard, 25

Siegel, Jeffrey, 81

Silverstein, Shel, 39

SLOP House, 54; see also Retirement

Small Business Administration, 146, 241

Smith, Logan Pearsall, 15

Software, Money Management, 92, 193, 234, 238

Sprouse, Mary L., 168

Standard & Poor's 500 Index, See S&P 500

Standared & Poor's Depositary Receipts (SPDRs), See S&P Depositary Receipts

Stanley, Thomas J., See *Millionaire Next Door, The*

Steadman, Hope, 26

Sterms, Linda, 157

Stevens, Mick, 1636

Stock Pickers' Success Plan, 124

Stock-picking, 113-121, 123, 124; see also Stocks

Stock-picking formulas, 117-21

Stocks, 51, 64, 80-82, 88, 113-125, 168, 202, 203, 208, 211, 212, 214, 215, 216, 217-18, 236, 244

Stocks: Categories, 217-18

Surprise Factor, 58

Swindoll, Charles, 35

Talking back, 38-41

Tax, 48-50, 55, 59-69, 90, 131, 134, 144, 159, 201-02, 214, 219, 220, 229

Tax Shelters, 49, 50, 83, 87, 144, 201, 212, 213-14, 247-48; see also 401(k)

Telephone solicitations, 167

Ten Minute Guide to Beating Debt (Abentrod), 136

Ten Painless Ways to Save, 148

Ten Safe Investments, 168

The Roaring 2000's, 91

Think and Grow Rich., 225

TIAA-CREF mutual funds, 51

Tightwad Gazette, 129

Time Shares, 163

Tips and Traps When Buying a Home, 74

Tornadoes 28

tornadoproject.com, 28

Torrey Pines Convalescent Center, 30

Treasury Bills, 168, 220, 236, 241

Trickle Up Program, 233

TRW (See Experian)

Umbrella Liability Policy, 56, 71, 93
University of Phoenix, 57
University of Redlands, 57
URLs for Websites, 239-41
USAA, 132

Valentine, Bill, 227
Value Line, 123
Vehicle Trap, 170-71
Villvicencio, Dennis, 158
Voices in your head, 39, 44

Wawanesa, 133
Websit Addreses (URLs), 239-41
What Color Is Your Parachute?, 147
WhatIf (Silverstein), 44
Where To Retire...America's Best and Most Affordable Places (Howells), 60
Who Am I, 28
Windfalls, 137-38

You By Design, 58
Young Entrepreneurs, Steps For, 109-10

Can I Help You?

Coleen Moore

*Writer * Speaker * Workshop Leader*

*Call me about doing a
"Money Makeover" for your group*

4323 Caminito del Diamante, #53
San Diego, CA 92121

(858) 457-5388 • phone
(858) 457-5488 • fax
Coleenm@pacbell.net • Email

QUICK ORDER FORM

Fax orders: (858) 457-5488. Send this form.
Telephone orders: (858) 457-5388.
E-mail orders: pointofviewpress@pacbell.net

Postal orders: Point-of-View Press, 4323 Cto. del Diamante, #53, San Diego, CA 92121 USA. Phone: (858) 457-5388

Please send _____ copies of *The Newbies' Money Guide* @ $14.95 each . (Call about special prices for orders of more than 10 books.)

I understand that I may return any of them for a full refund for any reason, no questions asked.

Please send more FREE information on:

_____ Speaking/Seminars   _____ Consulting

Name: _____
Address: _____
City_____State: ____ Zip: _____
Telephone _____
e-mail _____

Sales Tax: Please add 7.75% for products shipped to California addresses.
Shipping:
  US: $4 for the first book and $2 for each additional copy.
  International: $9 for first book and $5 for each additional (estimate).

Payment: Cheque_____ Money Order _____
Credit card orders through Amazon.com or
http://www.newbiesmoneyguide.com
pointofviewpress@pacbell.net